The
Professor of
Diddling

The Life and Times of Johnny
Briggs (1862-1902)

Colin H. Williamson

Contents

This book is dedicated to my wife Sandra and to my daughter Katie.

The Author

A life-long Lancashire cricket fan, Colin was born in Oldham, Lancashire in 1946 and started an apprenticeship in the construction trade upon leaving school. Studying in Further and Higher Education, he gained his first degree at Oxford and his Masters in Education from Leeds (studying at Huddersfield) in 1989. He is married with one daughter. He retired in 2002, moving to Southern Spain where he now lives.

Introduction

Johnny Briggs was unique, without equal or like. To set out the full facts and figures of the man who was christened John, but known variously as Johnny, Jack, "the boy" or W.G. Grace's baby, would not paint the full picture. However here is a brief pencil outline of the life and times of Johnny Briggs.

JOHNNY BRIGGS:

- Was a professional cricketer at the age of 13 years. Played for Lancashire at the age of 16 years 236 days. Was the first bowler to take 100 test wickets.
- Was the first cricketer to complete a test century and take a test hat-trick and, is the only player to complete this task in England and Australia test matches.
- Toured Australia six times.
- Took 7 for 17 in the first innings and 8 for 11 in the second innings of the second test in the 1888-1889 test series in South Africa. Match figures 15 for 28. On this tour Briggs played in all of the 19 matches on the tour taking an amazing 290 wickets at the cost of 5.62 runs per wicket.
- Had a walk-up (as opposed to a run-up) of 2 steps and was timed at 44 seconds for a 5 ball over.
- Bowled a record 630 balls in a match in 1897 at Old Trafford.
- Made 14,002 runs (18.27), 10 centuries, took 259 catches and 2,212 wickets (15.95) in his career.
- Took 100 wickets in a season on 12 occasions.
- Took 8 or more wickets in an innings on 14 occasions.

- Took 5 wickets in an innings on no less than 161 occasions. Took all 10 wickets against Worcester (55 runs) in 1900.
- In 1887 against a team of 15, took a double hat-trick (6 wickets with 6 consecutive balls) and had figures in this match of 8.2 overs, 7 maidens, 5 runs for 12 wickets. Was a partner with R Pilling when they combined to make Lancashire's record 10th wickets stand of 173. Briggsy scoring 186, this event took place whilst he was on honeymoon 2 days after his wedding in 1885.
- Was cursed with epilepsy.
- Died in Cheadle Royal Lunatic Asylum, diagnosed with Cerebal Paralysis of the Insane, not long after his 39th birthday.
- Internment was attended by over 2000 people, many more lining the route of the cortège. There was an "exceedingly large number of wreaths and messages of sympathy", including one from his personal friend the well-known comedian George Robey.

To any cricket enthusiast these facts and figures may well be amazing but they do little to explain Johnny Briggs the man. He was much more than a sum of all the parts. He was perhaps the greatest all-rounder that ever lived.

He was variously described as -

"a cheerful simple man who thought life great fun and adored cricket"

"he was a sort of India-rubber ball of a man, so enthusiastic, so good tempered and so amusing that it was impossible even for a man who had just been bowled by him not help liking him"

Johnny Briggs was simply the most popular player Lancashire had ever had, a popularity that spread through the country and indeed the cricketing world. He was a comedian and a joker on and off the field but like most humourists, he had his serious side, sometimes being very depressed because he had "many worries and troubles".

Johnny Briggs was greatly unique and uniquely great. Truly, as C.B. Fry stated about Johnny, he was a Professor of Diddling - diddling people out.

Colin H Williamson

1: The Early Years
(1862 to 1879)

JOHNNY BRIGGS WAS born on the 3rd October 1862, in Sutton in Ashfield, Nr. Mansfield, Nottinghamshire and was destined to become one of the greatest cricketers that ever lived. One of his many noticeable feats or records is that he was the first bowler to take 100 test wickets, and the only cricketer to score a test century and take a hat- trick in England v Australia test matches.

Neville Cardus when recalling how Briggs went to the wickets stated "he was, one thought like a happy boy going for a walk or rather in a quest of adventure. His eyes shone humour at you, his every moment was alive and youthfully alive. One has known dull days and dull cricket before the advent of Briggs, but he had just to show his face and the light passed over the field and with it companionable warmth. He was a man into whose body the humours of summer entered day by day, sunshine, wind and refreshing dews. No cricketer every lived who was so much the child of nature as Briggs".

His humanity and love of life was recognised by all who watched him and it would be a huge understatement to say that he was very popular. He was an easy going ever smiling little man who rarely took life or himself seriously. But life did not do Johnny any favours and he had a number of tragedies to overcome in his short eventful life, including epilepsy.

He was born into a poor home, his father James was 22 years old when Johnny was born, he had an older brother

Joseph Banner Briggs (Banner being his mother's maiden name) who was aged 4 years when Johnny was born.

His father worked as a stocking framework knitter but was soon himself to become a professional cricketer. His mother was illiterate, as shown by her "mark" on the birth certificate as opposed to a written signature.

Seven years later in 1870. After moving to Thicknell Earthwaite, Johnny's sister Sarah was born. It should be noted that when the family lived in the Cross Keys Public House at Appleton Widnes (1881) where James was the licensee, Sarah then 11 years old and at school was described to quote the terminology of the time as "Imbecilic or Idiot and Lunatic".

In 1873 another sister Alice was born, also whilst they were living in Thicknell Earthwaite and in 1875 a second brother arrived James Alfred. He moved to Widnes in Cheshire, where James Briggs became the professional at Widnes Cricket Club in 1876, and a year later he brought his household from Sutton to the centre of the chemical trade and then in 1880 a further son William Harold was born. By now the family was complete.

If fate dealt him a poor hand on various fronts, including his health, it certainly redressed the balance somewhat, with his cricketing ability, his birth place and a caring, loving and supportive father. Johnny was born in Sutton in Ashfield, in Nottinghamshire. Nottinghamshire at that time was the centre of cricketing interest and produced numerous cricketers of outstanding ability, many going on to play country cricket and indeed a number at test level, so cricket was the most important and encouraged sport at the time in that area.

His father was to provide all the help and encouragement he wanted and needed throughout his life. He recognised Johnny unique ability from an early age and being passionate about cricket himself coached Johnny and his brothers to a high level of skill. James went on to be a professional at Widnes and was so passionate about the game on retirement from Widnes he formed his own cricket team Briggs CC.

It was not uncommon for James to be seen practicing with Johnny as early as 5 am on a Spring or Summer morning when Johnny was about 8 years old. Johnny's father, James, was not averse to moving around the country to obtain cricketing positions with various clubs, not a common occurrence for the working man and his family in the early 1870s.

In the early days before compulsory education Johnny Briggs did not like the confines of the school room and "never went to school very much", stating that "it didn't seem much in my line". Johnny preferred the fresh air and the green fields, quite often he would run away to play cricket on the recreational ground (Lammas) in Sutton.

The lack of education did not seem to be any great draw back to Johnny for in later years he would recite the whole of Macbeth to his team mates during breaks for rain in test matches, and his love of fresh air was to stay with him throughout his life, for when Johnny travelled to and from Australia he was not very often found in his cabin on board ship being more content to "sleep on deck".

Johnny started work with his father in the stocking factory, and by the age of 10 years could "work a stocking frame fairly well", but as he stated "the stocking frame pleased me no more than the school desk", although he did at one time consider returning to the trade on retirement or if cricket failed him.

James Briggs played for the Ashfield Albion Club and in 1870 was engaged to play for Selkirk in Scotland; he was however two years later in 1872 engaged to play for the Hornsea

Club near Hull. James Briggs moved to Hornsea with his family in June 1872, his job description included "bowling to the club members in the afternoons on weekdays, playing for the club on Saturday" and also to "tend the ground (groundsman)".

When James Briggs arrived at Hornsea he brought his wife and his two sons with him. They lodged with Mr Webster in Hillerby Lane, Hornsea, living in the town in the summer and returning to Sutton for the winter months. His first game for Hornsea was against his home town Sutton. He scored 19 with the bat and took 5 wickets. In late August of that year James Briggs was awarded a benefit match. Although a large number of tickets had been sold previously to the match it was played in poor weather in front of a small crowd, so therefore not much money was raised. The match was drawn. This was unfortunate as it had been recorded in committee notes that "by his careful attention to his duties and his abilities as a cricketer and a groundsman he was held in high esteem". James Briggs was given another benefit the following season in which he took 8 wickets including 3 in 4 balls. In contrast to the 1872 benefit match it was a financial success. James Briggs finished at Hornsea the following season 1873 by taking 15 wickets for 3 runs each. His 3rd and last benefit match was again affected by rain, and was not as financially successful as the previous year. The Hornsea Gazette noted that Briggs "had given great satisfaction by the excellent wickets he has always had ready, whether for matches or practice".

Briggs moved on from Hornsea to play one season for Morley and one for Dudley but was asked to return for a special match. This was for the Hornsea Cricket Club v The Clown Cricketers. This type of match which was a mixture of reasonably competent cricket and clowning around in fancy dress, was popular for a while in the 1870s. The touring

"Clowns" had previously played matches at Kings Lynn and Northampton. James Briggs took 6 for 36 in 35 - 4 ball overs.

In the 1874 season Briggs was replaced at Hornsea by T Milnes, however the following season 1875, Hornsea Cricket Club looked for a replacement for T Milnes. They then employed John Briggs (Johnny) who amazingly was only 13 years old, when he arrived in Hornsea in April 1875. He was paid 25 shillings a week as the professional cricketer for Hornsea Cricket Club. Before becoming the professional he was spotted at Hornsea by W G Grace when he played there for the USEE (United South of England Eleven). During lunch break on one of the days W G Grace was in the nets practising when one of the Southern players persuaded James Briggs to put Johnny on to bowl against the famous Gloucester man (W G Grace), after a few balls by Johnny, W G seemed a little surprised at his wonderful bowling. Very soon he succeeded in taking the great man's wicket. James Briggs was told to take good care of his son as he "had all the qualities of making a good cricketer".

Johnny Briggs later recalled that "the Club did not want a full time professional and they thought I might do, though I could only bowl 18 yards. I was pretty straight but knew nothing about making the ball turn". At the end of the 1877 season, in September, Johnny Briggs left Hornsea and went to Widnes where his father was the professional cricketer. The Hornsea Gazette noted that "the committee intend to engage an older professional next year as Briggs had been by no means attentive as he should have been".

James Briggs retained the position of the professional at Widnes cricket club for the next 15 years. Young Johnny and his brother Joe were active in the sporting life of their adopted town apart from their cricket activities, they started an Association Football Club but this lasted only a one year, Johnny also played for a Widnes Rugby XV (the Widnes Club was one of the first to join the Northern Union when it succeeded from the Rugby Union in 1895). Johnny was a good full-back but also played in the three quarters for some games. In later years when he was contracted to Lancashire on a regular basis (1882) he broke his arm warming up before the Widnes and Sale match and therefore had to retire from Rugby at the request of the Lancashire committee. He was also a good billiards player and was "keenly attracted to that game".

James Briggs and his family moved to 8 Gladstone Street, Widnes, from which address he also sold cricket bats and sports equipment. In 1879 he was supplying cricket balls at 36 shillings for half a dozen. Since his wages in those days were only 48 pounds per year he needed the additional support of his shop. Widnes was and still is built around the chemical industry, the Rugby League teams nick name is the "Chemics" and many of the people that live in the surrounding area worked within the industry. In 1879, Widnes, it is true to say was a dirty smelly place full of chemical fumes, therefore many trips were organised so that the townsfolk could "temporarily escape the smoke fumes and smells of Widnes", for instance on 14th July 1879 the International Order of Good Templars (Star of Widnes Lodge) arranged a trip to Eastham (the Richmond of the Mersey) on the splendid fast sailing steamer Wasp at a fare of 1s and 3d, which included admission to the grounds at Eastham. The steamer left Westbank dock at 7.45 am sailing to New Brighton on one bank of the river Mersey and back via the line of docks on the other side. 500 trippers arrived at Eastham at noon and spent 6 and half hours there before the return sail to Widnes, the voyage was enlivened by the strains of the Good Templars brass band, the weather was showery during the day but the evening weather was delightful. Trips were also arranged by various Sunday schools who took children out of the smoke and smells for a few hours. In 1879, 130 Albert Road Wesleyan Sunday school scholars journeyed by cart and lorry to a field at Penketh. The Ditton Sunday school scholars were transported in similar conveyance to Pex Hill. The 200 Primitive Methodist scholars of Hutchingson Street would be conveyed into a pure atmosphere for a few hours to a field off Hale Road. The 400 scholars of Victoria Road Wesleyan Sunday school rode in conveyances lent by the Widnes Foundry Company to a field at Ditton. On the last two occasions a rainy evening compelled an early return, but the scholars of Milton Congregational Sunday School (350 of them) had a glorious fine day for their outing to Mr W H Kershaw's field at Ditton. It was to this type of environment that young Johnny arrived in 1879 and was their employed by the Messrs Pilkington Chemical works, in a place he did not particularly like to work, but as Johnny stated "cricket had more charms for me than chemistry".

Cricket was very strong in the Widnes and Merseyside areas and with the good rail communication network a number of clubs sprung up. The Merseyside teams included the Wirral down to the Chester area and there were a number of teams on the competition area. For example the 19th century records of the three early Southport clubs, Southport, Southport Alexander and Birkdale CC which eventually merged to become Southport and Birkdale CC showed that 137 different opponents, could be identified in the years 1859 to 1895. The map below shows the dates the various railways lines were opened and the years when the clubs were formed.

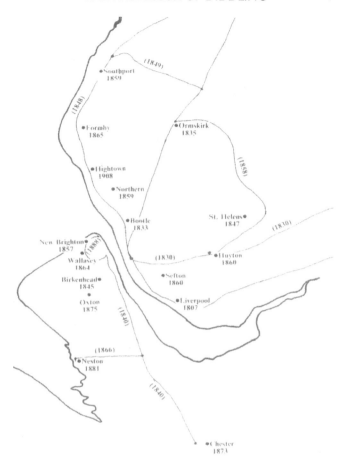

The railway network and the competition clubs.

Johnny's father had heard on the cricketing grapevine that the Anfield Club in Liverpool were looking for a professional for their team, so Johnny and his father lost no time in travelling to Liverpool to apply for the position. Johnny had injured one of his fingers at the chemical works but this did not stop him from "putting on kid gloves and attempting to play". Both James and Johnny Briggs bowled all afternoon to each other at the end of that day the Secretary approached them and said he would engage James. Whereas James smiled and told the secretary that it was Johnny that wanted the position and not him, the secretary replied that "he could not entertain the idea of employing Johnny for he was too young altogether".

Father and son soon departed and next headed for the Northern Club in Waterloo, Liverpool, but this time they were joined on their travels by Joe Briggs. They played a match for the Northern Club and were on the winning side. The Club spotted Johnny's potential and offered him the position of professional at the club. James Briggs stated that Johnny would not take less than 30s a week but in the end a compromise was reached and the deal was struck at 28s a week. The first time that Johnny played for Northern Club at Anfield, Liverpool, he got 8 wickets and scored 70 runs. In the return match against Anfield at the Northern Club ground he took 6 wickets and made 47 runs. Johnny stated that "because of the circumstances" (i.e. his refusal at Anfield) he and the secretary from Anfield had "many a laugh and talked about it since". There was a fading team photograph in which Johnny was pictured at the Northern Club on 8th August 1878 when the opponents were Southport Alexandra. Northern won by 28 runs in this low scoring match, Briggs taking 7 wickets.

Whilst at the Northern Club James Briggs always wanting his son to progress sent in an application to Nottingham CC, to see if Johnny could play for the Colts of that county, James was at first delighted when the reply was in the affirmative, however it transpired that although the Nottinghamshire Committee had agreed that Johnny should play for the Colts they would not pay any expenses. Both James and Johnny "did not see why they should go to Nottingham and back and pay their own expenses". Johnny Briggs never played for his native county.

Whilst playing in a benefit match in Liverpool he was spotted by R G Barlow, the Lancashire player who had a reputation for being a stonewaller, having batted right through an innings 50 times, including an innings of 5 not out in two and a half hours. Barlow then recommended Johnny Briggs to Sam H Swire of Lancashire who immediately put him on the ground staff. In the same year 1879 Johnny played for Lancashire Colts against the County Club which in practice was the Manchester Club and Ground. James Briggs was thunderstruck when Johnny was bowled out without scoring in the first innings and only got a single run in the second. He did however take six wickets in the second innings with his fast left handed deliveries. It should be noted that Johnny had not been converted to slow bowling at that time. A couple of weeks after the Colts match, in Manchester, Johnny Briggs was sitting in his lodgings at Seaforth, Liverpool when his landlady came in with a telegram for him. He ripped the telegram open to see it was a request for him to play for Lancashire against of all teams his native county Nottinghamshire. Johnny ran off to find the Secretary of the Northern Club Mr Molyneux and asked to be "let off for he had to play for his county". Mr Molyneux was delighted for young Johnny and stated they "he would certainly do so". Johnny Briggs made his debut for Lancashire against Nottinghamshire at Trent Bridge on 26th May 1879 aged 16 years and 236 days. To play your first match against a team of such standing as Nottinghamshire was indeed a severe test. This was not made any easier by the cold and cheerless weather throughout the 3 days fixture. Because of rain the day before the match, the pitch itself was in a "difficult" condition and having to face such bowlers as Alfred Shaw, Morley, Barnes and Flowers indeed was no mean feat. Briggs showed plenty of confidence and under trying conditions made the highest score for Lancashire that of 36. After the match the Nottinghamshire Captain Holden asked Johnny why he was not playing for his native county Nottinghamshire. Some of the Notts supporters also got on to Hornby the Lancashire Captain about pinching Johnny Briggs from them. He told them that "they should look after their own men themselves".

Johnny Briggs subsequently moved into the home of Barlow and the pair played together for Lancashire and England, they made such an impression that after a Lords test match, a London newspaper penned the following words

Thanks to you, we're dancing jigs,
Shrewsbury, Barlow and Briggs,
Who'll call England's cricket low
Briggs, Shrewsbury and Barlow,
Here's to your health, you glorious three,
Barlow, Briggs and Shrewsbury

Johnny Briggs continued to live with Barlow for 2 years during which time Barlow and Watson coached him in every department of the game. Barlow always considered that they were well rewarded for their pains and he knew that "Johnny Briggs would become one of the finest all round cricketers for his height 5ft 5inches that ever lived".

2: The Formative Years
(1880 to 1885)

JOHNNY BRIGGS WAS engaged by Lancashire from 1879. When one says 'engaged by Lancashire' in reality what that meant was that he was engaged by the Manchester Club and Ground. No other major city in England had so much influence over its county side. The Manchester Club paid the expenses of all county matches providing all home matches were played at Old Trafford. It employed the professionals who played for the county, it selected the county teams and the Manchester Club fielded all the county side. In fact it was the county side. So for Lancashire, read Manchester.

The City of Manchester was at that time increasing in size and prosperity brought about by the cotton boom. A number of the merchant gentry with money to spare and people to impress, used their influence and power to network within the Club. An Old Boys Club. It was no accident that during this period, expressions like "to play with a straight bat" and "it's not cricket", became common usage. The sentiments they echoed clearly reflected the upper class values which by this time dominated the game.

From his start at Lancashire, Briggs was much loved; his very nature endeared him to all who came in his presence, even the opposition. Cardus remembered him as a clown "Grimaldi among cricketers, a joker, a prangster, always ready for a laugh but with bulbous eyes and a thread of tragedy running through him". It was once recalled that in the years when clubs had very little money or assets it was not unusual for the wicket keeper to be the only player on the field wearing two pads, the batters had to make do with a single pad strapped to the leading leg. However Johnny Briggs "for a lark" proceeded to arrive at the crease with the pad firmly fitted to his back leg. When his attention was called to the fact he replied that "he thought he was batting at the other end".

In 1881 Alfred Shaw, who later was to take tours to Australia with Lillywhite and Shrewsbury, organised a strike among the Nottinghamshire professionals. Seven of the Nottinghamshire team demanded a formal Contract of Employment which would guarantee them an automatic Benefit on completion of an agreed span of years. Their action was seen as anarchy and the offenders were immediately dropped by the Nottinghamshire committee. Eventually there was reconciliation but the power had moved firmly into the hands of the committee.

When this strike was taking place in Nottinghamshire, Richard Daft from Nottinghamshire was playing in Manchester and asked Johnny whether he would consider playing for the county of his birth. Briggs replied "that Lancashire had always looked after him well whereas Nottinghamshire had done nothing of the kind". Briggs referred Daft to Hornby the Lancashire Captain who it is fair to say was not pleased and stated firmly that "it was not right for Daft to try and make Briggs leave Lancashire".

Lancashire 1881. Standing: A. Watson, J. Crossland,
R. Pilling, (unknown), G. Nash or W. Robinson. Seated:
(unknown), A.N. Hornby, (unknown), (unknown).
On ground: R.G Barlow, J. Briggs *(Lancashire CCC)*.

Briggs improved his figures that season (1881), this was
the year Lancashire won the championship. He took part
in every match during the season, scoring 52 and 39 against
Surrey, 40 not out against MCC and ground where a brave
display by Briggs, against the attack of Shaw and Morley
won the game for Lancashire by 2 wickets. That season he
also scored 40 v Kent, 33 v Derby and 31 v Notts. and had
2 knocks of 24 against Yorkshire. His total number of runs,
for that season were 376 from 21 innings at an average of
17.9.

Always a keen student of the game, Johnny would have
been aware of the events that occurred in the only test match
played that year at the Oval, when England were bowled

out in the second innings for 77 when chasing 85. This was the first time that an Australian team had defeated the full strength England side, in England, and on the following day the Sporting Times came out with their now famous obituary.

In Affectionate Remembrance
OF
ENGLISH CRICKET,
WHICH DIED AT THE OVAL
ON
29th AUGUST, 1882,
Deeply lamented by a large circle of sorrowing friends and acquaintances.

R. I. P.

N.B.—The body will be cremated and the ashes taken to Australia.

In the following winter 1882-83 the Hon. Ivo Bligh took a team to Australia and three test matches were played there. Australia won the first match by 9 wickets but England won the next two, and so secured the rubber. At the end of the third match some ladies burned a stump and sealed the ashes in an urn, presenting it to Hon. Ivo Bligh, later Earl Darnley. The urn was his private property until his death in 1927 when it was bequested in his Will to the MCC.

Johnny Briggs was just learning his trade in these days and in later years when asked what was the "chief piece of advice" you would give to a young bowler replied with the advice he was given in his earlier years, that was "to take care of himself and to be in bed by 11 o'clock, otherwise he may feel pretty sure that before very long he would drop out of first class cricket". He also added that "one of the great pit falls in the way of a young bowler, is the danger that he may become puffed up by too much praise"; he also stated that he "had seen many a promising young fellow ruined by this".

Briggs was under the watchful eye of Mr Hornby who taught him many lessons and on one occasion Briggs remembered he was fielding against Nottinghamshire, at cover-point, with instructions from his captain Mr Hornby to "cross over when a left hand batsman came in". The next man who came in was of course left handed but there was only one ball of the over remaining, Johnny stated "the square leg who ought to have crossed over motioned to me to take his place while he took mine". After the final bowl of the over was bowled, Hornby went across to Johnny and said "I say Briggs if I want my field changed I will change it myself". Briggs noted that "he was perfectly right too, always very strict, very stern and very kind".

On another occasion Hornby was disgusted with the way the Nottinghamshire batsmen played the break ball with their legs instead of with the "implement of defence". When Briggs faced the "Lacemen" next he also took to using the same method of defence. After his innings Hornby made it quite clear to Briggs that he did not like the use of these tactics and that he "would leave him out of the Lancashire Eleven if he ever played the 'Nottingham Game' again". Hornby also looked after Johnny off the field and knowing Johnny and his attraction to accidents or mishaps and his love of pranks told him firmly "not to patronise the switchback railway at the Jubilee Exhibition in Manchester".

In 1882 Lancashire had a powerful side with the likes of Hornby, Barlow, Watson plus the amateurs Vernon Royle and Alan Steel. But with Briggs not yet in his prime Lancashire's middle order was a trifle unsettled. The Rev. Vernon Royle was the best cover point of his day and with the youthful Briggs and the older Barlow on the off-side it was a fine fielding team. In fact in the early days Briggs was played as much for his fielding than anything else.

The successful Lancashire team of 1881 that included Briggs was subject to attack on two fronts a year later. The first was the accusation of "throwing". It was only in the 1860s that bowling with the arm above shoulder level had been legalised and there were several bowlers "bowling spontaneously and primitively and whose actions were technically illegal". The Lancashire bowlers Alex Watson and George Nash were under grave suspicion but the real target for the accusers was John Crossland probably the fastest bowler in England at that time. A huge proportion of Crossland's victims were clean bowled but there was little doubt his action was questionable.

The second problem which also involved Crossland was to do with residential qualifications. Lancashire were accused of using professionals drafted in from outside the county, this was positively illegal in those days. Nottinghamshire had drawn the MCC's attention to Crossland's residential qualifications, suggesting that he lived in Nottinghamshire in the winter months. At first the MCC came down in Crossland's and Lancashire's favour but acting on further information received from rates and rents collectors, a village postman and the county squire stating that Crossland had indeed lived in his native county Nottinghamshire from October 1884 until April 1885 they then reversed their decision and disqualified him.

The dispute between Nottinghamshire and Lancashire then became acrimonious and Lancashire sent a Christmas card to Trent Bridge in the form of cricketing rules, supposedly drawn up by Nottinghamshire. The rules involved Lancashire batsmen using broom-handles, their bowlers being refused permission to bowl, no stumps to be used, the umpires appointed must be strictly Notts men and Nottinghamshire refusing to finish the game should defeat loom. Nottinghamshire replied stating that "the only rules necessary" for Lancashire players is that they should neither have been born or reside in Lancashire, and also that Sutton in Ashfield men would have preference.

It should be noted that both Crossland and Briggs were

natives of Sutton. In fact Nottinghamshire dropped their fixtures with Lancashire from 1884 to 1886 because as they put it "grave doubts about the fairness of the bowling of two players".

1882 and 1883 had seen some decline in Lancashire's supremacy; in 1883 they did at one time seem set for another championship but fell apart in the second part of the season. It was at Old Trafford that year when Yorkshire ended Lancashire's hopes of another championship beating them by 8 wickets. It was then that Johnny Briggs took up slow bowling for it was "too much to do for a youngster to bowl fast". Briggs noted that "I have found too that I could break a bit". Johnny stated that "Alex Watson who was then the boss at Old Trafford advised me to go on with it", and that "Dickie Barlow was very good in that way also, he recommended me to keep to slow bowling". Johnny complemented his mentors by stating that "both Watson and Barlow were very kind to me and other young players" and added "some professionals are just the reverse".

To offset the troublesome and dismal Crossland affair, Johnny Briggs started to emerge during the 1883-1884 season as a slow left hand bowler of great potential as well as a more than valuable bat. It was recorded in Lillywhite's annual about Johnny Briggs performances in 1882 that he "has not come up to expectation in batting during the season. He is nevertheless a good cricketer being a useful left hand bowler and a splendid field at cover point". However concerning his 1883 performance they wrote "an excellent little cricketer, batted well this season, good change bowler and splendid field at cover point". The publication also noted that year that Briggs weight had gone up from 9 stone 10 pounds to 10 stone 6 pounds. Briggs opened the 1884 season in brilliant form scoring 74 against the MCC and ground at Lords. In his next match against Derbyshire his batting was described as "particularly vigorous", when he made 112 out of the teams total of 172. He played well all season and the performances of note were 75 not out in a total of 170 against Yorkshire in Allen Hills benefit match. He played in all four matches against the Australian touring team, the Lancashire match, the Players at Sheffield and the Oval and was a representative for the North at Manchester, he was also elected as one of the players against the Gentlemen at the Oval, this being his debut in this important fixture.

Johnny improved his performance so much in 1884 that he was selected for the 1884-1885 James Lillywhite's and Alfred Shaw's team to tour Australia leaving in the September of that year. On this tour Lillywhite acted purely as an umpire whilst Alfred Shaw did not play in any major matches and in fact managed the team.

Shaw noted later about the touring team that "a better side than this in both defence and attack could not then and am certain could not now be chosen from the ranks of English cricketers".

The team Shaw and Shrewsbury took to Australia in 1884-85, photographed in Sydney. The players are as numbered: 1 M. Read, 2 G. Ulyett, 3 W. H. Scotton, 4 R. Peel, 5 Joe Hunter, 6 W. Attewell, 7 A Shrewsbury, 8 A. Shaw, 9 W. Barnes, 10 J. Lillywhite, 11 W. Flowers, 12 J. Briggs, 13 W. Bates.

The touring side set sail from Plymouth on 19th September 1884 on the SS Orient, and arrived at Adelaide on 29th October of that year, this was in fact a day before the Australian team returning from the tour of England docked at Melbourne on the SS Mirzapore. The tour was to Egypt and Australia. The team were scheduled to have stopped at Naples on the way but this was cancelled due to an outbreak of cholera in the Italian City. They continued and arrived at Port Said on 30th September. They played a combined Army and Navy side on a matting wicket and a number of the party then went on a site seeing tour of the Pyramids and Cairo in the company of Thomas Cook, the head of the travel firm of that name, who had arranged the tour up the Nile.

Including the match played at Suez the touring party were to play 34 matches in total including 5 test matches, a daunting task for such a small squad.

On arrival at Adelaide, the team was greeted with the distressing news of Fred Morley's death. This was particularly depressing for some team members who were personal friends of Morley. Fred Morley was a member of the 1882-1883 touring team when on the long sea journey to Australia approx. 360 miles out of Colombo their ship collided with a sailing vessel. During the accidental collision Morley suffered a broken rib and although carried on with the tour in great pain, he never really recovered from this accident.

This tour was the first of Johnny Briggs six tours to Australia. He made his test debut in the first test which was the first test match ever played at the Adelaide Oval. It was already the 9th match of the tour and started on 12th December.

Alfred Shaw's team to Australia 1884-85. Standing: R. Peel, W. Barnes, J. Hunter, W. Attewell, J. Lillywhite jr (umpire), J. M. Read, (unknown), (unknown), W. Bates. Seated: A. Shrewsbury (captain), A. Shaw (manager), W. H. Scotton. On ground: W. Flowers, G. Ulyett, J. Briggs.

Johnny's debut test was not such a notable event for him, he was unwell and although he played, he did not bowl in the match and was caught behind the wicket by Blackham off the bowling of Palmer for a single run in his only visit to his crease. Johnny's illness was offset by the fact that the Australians had a somewhat weakened team. Spofforth's was absent through the death of a relative, Midwinter was missing with lung trouble, and Giffen was ill with lumbago. England did however win by 8 wickets, Australia batting first making 243 and then 191 England's first innings amounted to 369 with the 67 runs required to win being knocked off for the loss of 2 wickets. On the 2nd day of this match there was a violent dust storm which forced the players to lie down flat to avoid them being suffocated by the dust. The local forecasters claimed that the dust storm heralded rain and sure enough on the 3rd day the ground was flooded. England despite having the worst of the pitch won by 8 wickets.

The second test started on New Year's day 1885 and was a totally different match from Briggs point of view. There was a disagreement between the authorities and the Australian players. The Australians demanding 50 per cent of the profits from the match. Shaw had offered 30 per cent plus 20 pounds a man but this was still refused. The Victorian Cricket Authorities were acting as selectors, therefore disqualified all the Victorian players and made a clean sweep of all those who played in the first test at Adelaide. This was unfortunate for J M Blackham as he had already played in the first 17 test matches ever played. There were debuts in this match for the Australians -

W Bruce, A H Jarvis, A P Marr, S Morris, H Musgrove, R J Pope, W R Robertson, J W Trimble and J Worrall.

The Australian team was therefore for all intent and purposes a second eleven. For Morris, Pope, Marr, Musgrove and Robertson it was to be their only test. The match was unusual in the fact that it was the first time, three players from the same county - Shrewsbury, Scotton and Barnes of Northamptonshire, occupied the first three places in the English batting order.

England's score was 194 for 5 when Briggs went in at 4.45 pm, but by 6.00 pm he had scored 65 runs. His first 50 runs taking him one hour. England faltered somewhat after that and were reduced to 204 for 7. Briggs however was still there and was "jumping out like Shrewsbury to the slows, but keeping the ball down well" hitting "cleanly and hard". At the close of play on the first day England had recovered to 303 for 9, thanks mainly to Johnny Briggs who was still there on 65 not out.

On the second day it took the Australians another 1 hour

and a quarter to wrap up the English innings, Briggs completed his century in 2 hours and was to go on to reach 121 in 2 and a half hours before being brilliantly caught at deep square leg. He gave only two chances in his innings, one at long off when he was 95 and the one at slip when 117, both off the bowling of Morris. More telling of his knock is that it contained only 11 singles, 2 in reaching 53 and 6 in total reaching 101. England finished on 401 all out. Australia batted well in reply and ended the second day on 151 for 3. Soon after lunch on the third day however they had slumped to 203 for 7. When Jarvis and Worrall put on 73 for the eighth wicket, they had an excellent chance of saving the follow on.

It was then that Briggs took a fine catch running backwards from mid-on to dismiss Jarvis. Worrall was bowled soon after leaving Bruce high an dry, the Australians were bowled out for 279 and then 126 in the second innings. England therefore had won by 10 wickets. Briggs again did not bowl in this match.

The third test at Sydney. Briggs scored 3 in the first innings and one in the second. In the fourth test he scored 3 and 5 respectively and in the fifth he made 43 runs in his only knock. On 9th and 10th March in between the third and fourth test matches, the party took a detour and played one match in Wellington, New Zealand. In this match with the locals batting, two of them got themselves into somewhat of a mix up with their running between the wickets. So much so that the two ended up in the middle of the wicket together. The ball was returned to Briggs who immediately removed the bails, he promptly then threw the ball to George Ulyett, standing at the other end. Ulyett just as quickly removed the bails at the other end. The batsmen then asked Briggs if they were both out, Briggs retorted that "of course you a both out".

Both batsmen made their way to the pavilion. Shrewsbury then told one of them to return back to the crease which of course was the correct decision. Briggs bowled very little on the tour in fact the most used bowler on the tour Bobby Peel bowled 663.2 overs with 346 maidens, 673 runs and 23 wickets at an average of 29, contrasting this to the figures of Johnny Briggs who bowled 8 overs, 3 maidens, 13 runs and no wickets.

Johnny's love of the outdoors and sense of adventure got him into numerous scrapes on the tour. In Narabra, New South Wales, Briggs went horse riding and on one occasion got off the horse the wrong way i.e. left handed, the horse proceeded to kick Johnny towards the edge of a precipice, he was injured but that did not deter him from trying a second time at a later date. This time, while all the team stood watching, the horse bolted, Johnny tried hard to slow down the run-away horse, he eventually succeeded, controlling the horse, unfortunately the horse stopped very abruptly but Johnny did not, he continued over the horses head into mid-air before crashing to the ground face first, Johnny never did anything by halves and as he was smoking a pipe at this time its stem was forced into the roof of his mouth. Before falling unconscious, he requested his watching team mates to immediately remove the pipe stem from his mouth, a somewhat bloody request they reluctantly agreed to. Briggs was unconscious for 4 hours after the incident and it was first reported that he had been killed in the accident. It was said that his face was so bruised that looking at himself in the mirror he "did not recognise the reflection". If ever there was an accident waiting to happen it was Johnny Briggs, accident prone would be an understatement. Alfred Shaw later stated that "he was glad to get Briggs home alive, from that tour". As stated beforehand, England had left Plymouth on 19th September 1884, reaching Australia on 29th October the same year. The last match finished on 6th April 1885, they had played 34 matches and had travelled from Adelaide to Melbourne to Sydney, and then back to Melbourne again, either by boat or train, the trains being very uncomfortable and slow. It was said the England team used to get off and run alongside the train for exercise before remounting again.

They arrived back in England about the middle of May in time for the 1885 domestic cricket season. The players received good remuneration for their long tour, each receiving 300 pounds, plus a number of prizes for best performances in various matches, two of which included shares in a goldmine which the players auctioned off.

1885 was a momentous year for a number of reasons; it was then that all the years of hard work started to payoff for Johnny. His early morning practice at Sutton, his journeying throughout the land, and his continuous striving for perfection were at last starting to pay dividends. He himself when asked when did he meet with success in bowling stated that "not until 1885 when I was able to do a bit both ways, I had slowed down and got a good many wickets with a curly one from the off, though it was more or less a matter of chance where it was to pitch".

Johnny was completing his apprenticeship, but he already knew he had much more to learn to become a really great bowler. He acknowledged this when he stated that "if a man really wants to improve, there is always something fresh to learn, no matter how good he may be". Johnny's improvement can be seen from his Lancashire bowling figures from the years 1881 to 1885.

Year	Overs	Maidens	Runs	Wickets
81	4	0	7	2
82	67.2	27	108	6
83	48.2	16	90	1
84	255.2	126	402	18
85	666.3	335	951	81

These figures included a remarkable 9 for 29, against Derbyshire, all 9 being taken on the afternoon of the second day of the match when Derbyshire were 87 for 9 at the close of play. Briggs chance of taking all 10 wickets was quickly ruined the next morning when Watson opened the attack and bowled Bill Eadie with his first delivery.

From that year Johnny Briggs became established as a bowler, for 11 years in succession 1887 to 1897. He was never to obtain less than 114 wickets in a season. His highest number of victims during those years were 160 wickets in 1888, 158 wickets 1889, 166 wickets in 1893 and 165 wickets in 1896.

It should be noted here that the Crossland "throwing controversy" was still rumbling on in 1885, and Lancashire quite rightly continued to support their player. Lord Harris from Kent was one of his main accusers. It was rumoured that if Crossland or Nash were put on to bowl when Kent played Lancashire in the first match of the season at Old Trafford his Lordship would demonstrate. However when Lord Harris went out to bat on the opening day he was given a good ovation from the 12,000 plus crowd. The Manchester Guardian described what happened next

"Lord Harris played the first and second balls of the over with ease, but the third completely spread-eagled his wicket. The sight was too much for the crowd and the scene which followed showed that Crossland was regarded as having had his revenge in a manner which could hardly have been calculated. People seemed fairly beside themselves with delight. Hats and coats were thrown up and one enthusiast actually waved his coat from the top of one of the stands".

Because of the problems with Crossland's action, Lord Harris wrote a long letter of complaint to the Lancashire committee and gave the return fixture away, at Kent, stating that they would not play Lancashire again that season. The Lancashire Secretary Sam Swire wrote back on Monday 29th June 1885 answering Lord Harris's complaints. Lancashire might well have saved their breath and the time of the Secretary, Crossland had already played his last game for the Club two days earlier.

Late in 1884, before going on tour Briggs had moved his place of dwelling from 3 Gladstone Street, Widnes, to the home of Mr and Mrs Burgess at 30 Frederick Street, Widnes. On the 18th July 1885, the following article appeared in the Widnes Weekly News -

"The Marriage of John Briggs the well-known Lancashire Professional Cricketer to Miss Alice Burgess of Widnes took place in a quiet manner at the Parish Church, Farnworth on Tuesday. The service was performed by the Rev. George Bond in the presence of a small number of people. The newly married pair, after partaking of breakfast, went to Manchester where they intend residing until the conclusion of the cricket season, that year. The groomsmen at the altar were Pilling, Barlow and Watson the three professional cricketers".

Four stalwarts: R. Pilling, A. Watson, A. N. Hornby, R. G. Barlow. *Lancashire Cricket Club.*

Briggs married Alice Burgess but he was also at that time "wedded to cricket", for he played at Aigburth, Liverpool against Surrey the following day whilst still on honeymoon. On the first day of this match C E Horner from Surrey said to Hornby that "after the wedding festivities Briggs won't be of much use today, for it had been a tremendously fine party". At the end of the first day of the match Johnny Briggs was 18 not out with the Lancashire total standing at 186 for 8 wickets. The following day with only 5 runs added to the overnight total Alex Watson was out. Pilling then arrived at the crease to join Briggs; they proceeded to make a total of 173 runs for the last wicket, a record last wicket stand in first class cricket for Lancashire. Briggs total contribution was 186 runs and Pilling 61 runs. The Rev. George Bond, the vicar of Farnworth, was a friend and a devout admirer of Johnny and never missed a county match either at Manchester or Liverpool; it was the Rev Bond who had officiated at Johnny's wedding earlier in the week. When Johnny was smashing the Surrey bowling all over the Aigburth ground he was the most delighted spectator.

He could not stop himself repeating and with ever increasing emphasis the words "the little beggar, I only married him on Tuesday". Hornby the Lancashire captain was heard to remark that he wished "Briggs could always be on honeymoon", and that "I'd be married every day if I could bat as Briggs as done today".

There may have been a wedding that year but there was also an important arrival, after a gestation period of nearly 23 years Grace's baby, the boy, saw the light of day. Luckily for the cricketing world the boy was never to grow up, he was to be called "a Child of Nature", "a Flannel Fool". He was always to be happy go lucky, eccentric in a way, and casual to the point of waywardness. He was always a joker, a prankster, always ready to laugh. A player of humour as well as skill. He was also described as a "perfect cricketer", a "gay deceiver", a man when bowling would be "courteous yet deadly, greedy but never hungry". He was to set standards beyond reproach and was to have a dynamic impact on the game he loved.

Johnny Briggs emerged in 1885 after 6 years on Lancashire's books. He was to be much loved, throughout the cricketing world from Manchester to Melbourne and for the next 15 years, Johnny Briggs was to ply his trade throughout the world and was to become one of the greatest cricketers of all time.

43

3: The Impact Years
(1886 to 1888)

THE 1886 SEASON was a disappointing one for Lancashire although they finished third in the Championship, their batting was weak and they failed to find a fast bowler to replace Crossland. The team was rescued time and time again by the three main bowlers Watson, Barlow and Briggs. There were also complaints about the make-up of the team and all was not sweetness and light amongst the professionals. Lancashire won 5 and lost 5 putting them third behind Nottinghamshire and Surrey in the championship. Briggs however did score 107 against Kent at Old Trafford, 76 v Surrey, 72 v Gloucester and 53 v Sussex that season. Amongst his bowling figures that year for Lancashire in the first innings against Essex he took 5 for 13, and in the second 4 for 34. Against Gloucester at Old Trafford 7 for 50, and against Yorkshire in the only championship match ever played at Dewsbury, Yorkshire he took 5 for 37.

In those days players were not given a full benefit season as happens today but a single Benefit match. The player himself choosing which match he wanted for his benefit. It would be a big named team that could attract support and in those days more often than not would have been Nottinghamshire. Lancashire granted Barlow a benefit match in 1886 and the rift between Nottinghamshire and Lancashire had been healed by that time so Barlow chose the Nottinghamshire match because they had been Champions for the last four seasons and the match would draw a large and appreciative audience. Over 27,000 people attended the match over three days and over 1,000 pounds was raised for Barlow.

Lancashire had a poor season but nevertheless had the distinction of supplying four players for the England team at Old Trafford for the first test match against Australia, these being Barlow, Briggs, A G Steel and Pilling. There was no Test Selection Board or committee in those days and it fell upon the host committee to choose the test team, for example if the match was played at Trent Bridge the Nottinghamshire committee would pick the team, the Lancashire committee therefore picked the team for the first test at Old Trafford. The match started on 5th July 1886. The Australian tour of that year was organised for the first time by the Melbourne Cricket Club but it was seen very early that it was going to be an ill-fated tour; they were not a happy squad and quarrels developed from the start of the tour. The batting lacked Murdock, McDonnell, Bannerman and Horan. Bad weather had restricted their playing time on the tour and they recorded only a single victory in May. In June a hard drive from Lord Harris injured Spofforth, the Australian main bowler and in July Bonner was also injured. An experienced captain under the circumstances would have had difficulty maintaining moral so the novice captain Scott had very little chance of doing so. Scott in later years became a pioneering Doctor in the Bush and also Mayor of Scone. He died of typhoid contacted on one of his adventures to a remote outpost. A hospital was named after him after his death. England won by 4 wickets and it was Barlow that took the honours with his second innings bowling figures of 52-24-44-7. For some unknown reason Briggs did not bowl in the match but he did have the satisfaction of scoring the winning run at 5.40 pm on the last day. In a somewhat mirrored image, for Johnny the first and second tests were similar regarding his involvement to the first and second test in Australia in 1884, little of note in the first but greater impact in the second. Briggs fame as a bowler outside Lancashire really dated from the date of this match.

ENGLISH & AUSTRALIAN CRICKETERS
GREAT MATCH, ENGLAND v. AUSTRALIA, PLAYED AT LORD'S CRICKET GROUND, LONDON, 19th, 20th, 21st JULY, 1886
SCORES ENGLAND 1st INNINGS 353. AUSTRALIANS 1st INNINGS 121, 2nd INNINGS 126
ENGLAND WON BY AN INNINGS AND 106 RUNS

The second test was to be played at Lords starting on 19th July 1886 the match was scheduled for three days and the combination of Shrewsbury's batting and Briggs bowling was to prove decisive to the outcome of the match. England decided to bat first on a perfect wicket but within 15 minutes it had started to rain and play was held up for 85 minutes, this shower of rain changed the complete character of the wicket, so much so that the wicket threatened to become almost unplayable with the ball kicking and turning viciously. The early play saw Scotton, Read and Steel all return to the pavilion. Barnes joined Shrewsbury at 4.40pm when the wicket was at its worst and they both played magnificently to steer England from 119 for 4 to 202 for 4 at the close of play. Shrewsbury went on make a masterly 164 in England's total of 353. Australia had a strong batting attack and when Scott and Jones put on 45 runs with little trouble it looked as if England would be in for a long day, it was then that the English captain A G Steel tossed the ball to his Lancashire team mate Johnny Briggs. Briggs immediately had an impact, dismissing both openers with the score at 52. Steele himself caught Bonner and Griffiths and by the time the Australians had amassed 67 runs, 6 wickets had fallen. Briggs had the batsmen in all kinds of difficulties on a number of occasions and despite a rally from the tail-enders, Australia were dismissed for 121. Briggs figures were 34 22 29 5. When the Australians batted again, on the same day, Briggs took another wicket late on, the visitors finishing on 12 for 1 at the close of play on the second day. The wicket improved overnight and a fine stand by the overnight batsmen encouraged the Australians and their hopes of batting throughout the day and obtaining a creditable draw were increasing over by over. However when Briggs was brought on at the Pavilion End when the score was 76 for 2, the end was not far off. Briggs bowled 38.1 overs, 17 of which were maidens, 45 runs were taken off him but he took 6 wickets. The Australians were dismissed for 126 in the second innings, England winning by an inning and 106 runs going two nil up in the three match series. Briggs took 11 wickets for 74 runs in this match.

For the third test at the Oval on the 12th, 13th and 14th August the Surrey authorities wisely decided to leave well alone and play the successful team from Lords.

W G Grace completely dominated the first innings of this

match and when he was the second man out with England's score at 216 his contribution was 170 runs. Grace was helped by his opening partner Scotton who at one time went 67 minutes without scoring, Shrewsbury and Read added 63 bringing the score to 279 for 2 by the end of play on the first day. England were in a strong position and the following day they went for quick runs. Read hit out and was caught on the boundary for 94 and Briggs scored 53 runs in what was described as a "typically busy innings", which enlivened the finish. The Australians went in at 4.10 pm on the second day and were all out by 6.00 pm for 68 runs. Lohmann was unplayable on his own pitch taking 7 for 36 and Briggs 3 for 28. Lohmann and Briggs bowled unchanged throughout this innings. The Australians had made 8 without loss when they batted again by the end of the second day. On the final day the Australians had been bowled out by 3.00 pm for 149. Lohmann again doing the damage with 5 for 68 ably assisted by Briggs 3 for 30. England won the match by an innings and 217 runs and the series three nil. The manner of the series win set England up for the fourth coming tour to Australia which was to leave 2 months later on the 18th September 1886.

The early tours to Australia were demanding on the tourists and it was not uncommon to play a vast number of games with long distances in between venues. However the tour did have its lighter moments. In the match at Cootomondra, Johnny noticed that at times they could not get any decisions at all from the Umpire (the Mayor of Cootomondra). The tourists managed to capture six of the opponents wickets for 20 runs. When Lohmann bowled a half volley on the off side, the batsman after giving the ball a "hard crack" in Johnny's direction, obviously not knowing Johnny's reputation regarding fielding started to run. Briggs picked up the ball cleanly and promptly returned it to the wicket keeper. Sherwin, who just as promptly removed the bails while the batsman were still along way from the crease, the appeal went up but all the mayor could say was "well it's doosed marvellous, the best bit of fielding I have ever seen in My life". A repeat appeal resulted in the same response and they never did get the decision. The next ball Lohmann bowled was very wide indeed and this was all too much for Johnny for he stated that he "sat down and laughed till I nearly cried".

Some of the fixtures on this tour were against opposition of greater numbers for example v XVIII of Parramatta, XX of Ballarat and the XXII of Lithgow and so on. When playing against these kind of numbers they threw up some remarkable figures, one of these matches the one against Lithgow on the 8th and 9th December was a case in point. It had rained for four days before the match and the square was under water so a strip of matting was placed on the higher ground resulting in a short boundary on one side which was then deemed to count for two runs. The eleven of England batted first and made 80 runs on a difficult wicket, the 22 of Lithgow made only 18 runs in reply Briggs taking 10 wickets for 7 runs. England faired a little better in their second innings amassing a total of 42 runs. When the 22 of Lithgow returned to bat for the second time, they were all out for 27, Briggs taking 17 of the 22 wickets for 13 runs in this innings. England won by 77 runs. Briggs match analysis was therefore 27 wickets for 20 runs. The party next took to the train rather than the usual sea journey from Adelaide to Melbourne, this was a long journey taking 28 and a half hours.

The party which visited Australia in 1886-87 photographed in Melbourne. This was the team led by Shaw, Shrewsbury and Lillywhite. Back row: W Flowers, A. Shrewsbury, G. A. Lohmann, W. Gunn, W. Barnes, T. M. Read. Seated: W. Bates, A. Shaw, J. Lillywhite (umpire), M. Sherwin, W. H. Scotton, R. G. Barlow. Front row: J. Briggs.

There would be only two test matches on the tour; the first test was played at Sydney on 28th, 29th and 31st January 1887. This was to be the seventeenth match of a 29 match tour. The second test was also played at Sydney on the 25th, 26th and 28th February and 1st March, and was the twenty third match of the tour.

LILLYWHITE, SHAW AND SHREWSBURY'S 1886-
1887 TOUR OF AUSTRALIA – ITINERARY

Depart Plymouth 18th September 1886, Arrived Adelaide 29th October 1886

Oct	30th-31st and 1st	v	South Australia (Adelaide)
Nov	6th, 8th, 9th, 10th	v	Victoria (Melbourne)
	12th, 13th	v	XVIII Paramatta (Paramatta)
	19th, 20th	v	New South Wales (Sydney)
	26th, 27th	v	XVIII of Goulburn (Goulburn)
	29th, 30th	v	XXII of Cootamundra (Cootamundra)
Dec	3rd, 4th, 6th	v	XVIII Sydney Juniors (Sydney)
	8th, 9th	v	XXII Lithgow (Lithgow)
	10th, 11th, 13th	v	New South Wales (Sydney)
	17th, 18th, 20th, 21st, 22nd	v	1886 Australians (Melbourne)
	23rd, 24th	v	XVIII Geelong (Geelong)
	27th, 28th, 29th	v	XX of Ballarat (Ballarat)
Jan 87	1st, 2nd, 3rd	v	1886 Australians (Melbourne)
	7th, 8th, 10th, 11th v	v	1886 Australians (Sydney)
	14th, 15th	v	1886 Australians (Sydney)
	17th, 18th	v	XVIII of Bathhurst (Bathhurst)
23rd, 24th		v	XXII of Orange (Orange)
	23rd, 24th	v	XXII of Bowral (Bowral)
	25th, 26th	v	XXII of Camden (Camden)
	28th, 29th, 30th	v	Combined Australia - 1st Test (Sydney)
Feb	4th, 5th	v	XXII of Narrabri (Narrabri)
	7th, 8th	v	XXII of Armidale (Armidale)
10th, 11th, 12th		v	XVIII of Newcastle (Newcastle)
	14th, 15th	v	XVIII of Singleton (Singleton)
	18th, 19th, 21st	v	New South Wales (Sydney)
25th, 26th, 28th, 1st		v	Combined Australia - 2nd Test (Sydney)
Mar	4th, 4th, 7th, 8th	v	Victoria (Melbourne)
	11th, 12th, 14th	v	XV of East Melbourne (Melbourne)
	15th, 16th	v	XVIII of Sandhurst (Sandhurst)
	24th, 25th26th	v	XV of South Australia (Adelaide)

Depart Adelaide 26th March 1887, Arrived Plymouth 8th May 1887

51

The touring party was restricted to a total of 13 members/ discounting Shaw (Manager) and Lillywhite (Umpire) only 11 members were available to play in the above matches.

The long journeys and the congested fixture list did not stop the touring party enjoying themselves with outside interests in their spare time. At Bathurst before the match on 14th January some members of the party decided to spend the night in the bush. About 11.00 pm at night, Shaw, Scotton, Read, Lohmann, Briggs and the organiser Mr Clarke, set off in a trap to travel about 8 to 10 miles through bush country. The path was very uneven with ruts in the road causing the trap to lean from one side to the other; Briggs was to comment later that he was "ready to jump out as he felt certain that the show was going over". The party eventually arrived safely at about 2.00 am and they had taken essential rations such as "beef, cigars and beer", and they set about pitching their tents. Briggs stated that "Scotton and myself nearly perspired away with working to get timber for lighting the fire", and of course only Briggs could continue that "when we did get it right it made such a bonfire that it nearly set the trees alight". When the fire was under control the "Billies" cooked the beef for the members and then they all fell asleep about 5.00 am. Clark, Read, Scotton and Briggs all slept in the tent and the others in the trap, although the mosquitoes limited the time they slept that night. The next morning they want kangaroo hunting "on foot with guns". They came across a number of kangaroos but hit none, Briggs stated that "it was fun to see Scott and Read hitting the trees and missing the kangaroos by yards", he concluded that "the sport was good but the results poor and that the night and day would live in his memory for many a long year as something novel".

The first test match was once again remarkable and one that Briggs had a role to play, a note of interest here is that it was the first time that a captain who had won the toss, (P S McDonnell, Australia) would invite the opposition to bat first in a test match. The start of the match was delayed because of another match (inter-colonial) had not yet finished. The first day's play did however start at 2.20 pm, when the inter-colonial match had been concluded. Australia bowled and particularly fielded brilliantly and had England in all sorts of trouble early on with 5 wickets down for 13 runs, 7 wickets down for 21 runs, they eventually reach a meagre total of 45, thanks mainly to 17 from Lohmann the only man to reach double figures. The England total remains the lowest in a test match between the two countries. When Australia batted they lost two quick wickets at 8 and 18 but passed the English total without any other alarms. They went on to reach 119 giving them a lead of 74. When England took the field a second time they faired not much better than in their first innings when at close of play on the second day they were reduced to 103 for 7 a slender lead of just 29 runs. The England tail wagged and with Briggs scoring 33 valuable runs, in a low scoring match, they managed to reach a respectable total of 184, this left the Australians 111 runs to win. However the English bowlers and Barnes in particular bowled brilliantly, Barnes figures being 46-29-28-6, and with the help of Lohmann 24-11-20-3, and a single wicket from Briggs 7-5-7-1, England bowled them out for 97. England winning by 13 runs.

In recognition of the part Briggs had played in England's winning of the two Test matches, he was presented with a Gold medal or medallion by the then Prince of Wales (later King Edward VII). This beautiful example of the silversmith's art was in the shape of a Gold Shield with a Royal Coat of

Arms at the top and inner shield with an inscription and the initials JB studied with seven diamonds. In between the diamond studied initials silhouetted in gold leaf was a solid gold cricket bat in miniature. In 1923, twenty one years after the death of Johnny Briggs this medallion was presented by Oliver Isherwood to the Lancashire Cricket Club President, at a private ceremony at Old Trafford. Unfortunately the medallion was stolen in 1930 and its present whereabouts are sadly unknown.

After the first test the touring party moved on to Narrabri. It was here that Briggs and Scotton went on a kangaroo hunting expedition again but this time on horseback.

The outing was organised by a local gentleman Mr Moseley. Briggs did call the venue Marribria but added that "he thought that was the name of the place but was no good with Australian names". Johnny also stated "that it was just as well the whole team did not go hunting as it just about knocked us up". It may be appropriate to use Johnny's words here concerning the expedition for a modern translation would not do justice to the event. Briggs revealed afterwards that "the horses didn't take much notice of the bridle they dodged the trees themselves and the trees in the bush are as thick as blackberries, so it was a case of sticking to the gee-gee back and let the hunting take its course. My horse sometimes would dodge the trees and let me have a branch straight in my face, so the best way was to lay close to the horse's neck even then some of the men had been left hanging from trees and the horse had gone on without its rider. This sort of wriggling circus riding was one of the features of up country sport and though was thanked out guests we rather wished we hadn't gone".

The tourists experienced wet weather during early February

and did not play at Yaas but they did have a very successful concert evening and were presented with a silver medal as a memento of their efforts. Another concert was held at Armidale and they actually received more money from the concert than they did from the cricket match. In the concert Barlow sang "What Only lips", and received an encore, they were all given a gold medal for their help with the concert and the collection on the night raised 85 pounds for the team.

They then went on to Sydney to play the second test on 25th February; the match itself was a fairly low key event with noticeable events influencing its outcome.

England were without Barnes, who in a hasty moment swung a punch at McDonnell the Australian captain, missed and hit a brick wall, thus ruling him out of the match. Barnes was replaced by Mr R Wood, who played one match for Lancashire, before emigrating to Australia. He was co-opted into the English side for this one and only Test and is probably the least known cricketer to represent England in an Ashes match.

In the match Johnny Briggs played "too short but merry knocks of 17 and 16", W Gunn played for England, batting in both innings, but also umpired for part of the match, but the main point of interest was Lohmann taking 8 for 35 in the Australian first innings, this being the first time any bowler had taken 8 wickets in a single test innings.

England batted first and recovered from 50 for 6 to make a credible 151. The Australian first innings reply totalled 84, 67 behind the England total. On England's second visit to the crease they struggled early on again at 73 for 5 but rallied to make 154, leaving the Australians 222 runs to win. With Briggs taking 3 for 31, Lohmann 2 for 52 and Bates 4 for 26 the Australians were bowled out on the morning of the fourth day for 150. England winning by 71 runs.

After this test the team were down to play East Melbourne at Melbourne, they rearranged this to play another match against combined Australian team but unfortunately a number of the Australian team, mainly the New South Wales contingent were unavailable, so they arranged another match with the addition of a few locals and played a match between the smokers and the non-smokers of the tour. In 1887 this match must have been one of the earliest examples of sponsorship and with the teams entering the field smoking cigars it is doubtful whether this sight would be seen ever again. Four companies agreed to put up prizes for the match, they were as follows -

1. The highest score on the smokers team - 500 cigars (SAQUI)

2. Best bowling on the smokers team - 500 cigars (Jacobs Hart and Co)

3. Highest score on the non-smokers team - 250 cigars (Kronheimer Co)

4. Highest individual score in the match - 250 cigars (Kronheimer Co) and

5. Best bowling in the non-smokers team - 200 cigars and trophy (White Co)

The wicket was a "belter, a batter's dream and a bowler's nightmare", the non-smokers piled on the runs, when they batted first, and Briggs was reported as saying to the umpire that "I believe one ball in the last over nearly broke a quarter of an inch". The non-smokers managed to amass a record 803 runs in 302.1 overs. Briggs' figures of 55.1-11-141-4 in context looked quite good and were enough to gain him the bowling prize for the smokers team. The non-smokers made 356 and 135 for 5 in the second innings of the drawn match. Scotton the Nottinghamshire batter was determined to secure the match ball as a souvenir. When the last ball of the match was bowled to him he played it gently towards point and ran after it to retrieve but Sherwin the non-smokers wicket keeper had the same idea for a memento and he too raced after the ball. Scotton had prior knowledge of the event and was therefore first to the ball. However the umpire had not called "over" and gave Scotton out "handled the ball"; Scotton was not too distressed as he had in his possession the match ball as a much treasured souvenir.

The team headed for England on 26th March on board the Massilia. On their way back the boat anchored at Colombo and seeing it was a glorious morning Briggs along with Gunn decided to cool off by having a morning swim in the bay. On arriving back on board after what was a most enjoyable swim, they were approached by the Quarter Master who informed them that the harbour was infested by sharks which constantly followed the boat for its refuge. Gunn later commented that "it is necessary to ask you to imagine the look we gave each other as we shook hands and retired to restore ourselves to our personal comforts". All members of the touring party returned fit and well and landed at Plymouth on 8th May 1887.

Johnny Briggs was a cricketing "nut" he was a "Martini" of a cricketer "Any time, Any place, Any where", and it was not long after the end of the demanding Australian tour that he was back on the field casting his magic spell again. On the 8th June 1887 Mr Hornby opened a private cricket ground next to his home at Parkfield, Nantwich, Johnny played in this opening match against a local fourteen combined from the neighbouring villages of Church Minshull and Minshull Vernon. It was in this match that Briggs took 6 wickets in successful balls, all bowled. The first five wickets fell to the last five balls preceding lunch and the six the first ball after lunch. Briggs recalled an incident during the match stating "I had bowled a yorker pitching between the middle and the off stump, the ball turned and went on to Watson at short slip, after removing a bail. Watson caught the ball and at once returned it to me, meanwhile Pilling had replaced the bail and I then pretended to carry on bowling again. The batsman looked around in bewilderment and said 'Well I could have sworn I was out', and was proceeding to bat again but I had to explain that we had been having a joke with him because there was a chance of me doing a record in bowling and he would have to go". Including the six wickets in six balls, his match analysis was 17 wickets for 16 runs, at one point claiming 11 wickets without conceding a single run.

His bowling figures for the match read as follows

First Innings, 8.2 overs, 7 maidens, 5 runs, 12 wickets

Second Innings 12 overs, 6 maidens, 11 runs, 5 wickets

Match Figures 20.2 overs, 13 maidens, 16 runs, 17 wickets

In addition to this he scored 96 runs out of a total of 262 when Mr Hornby's team batted.

Briggs could mix with anyone in cricketing terms and it was not long before he exchanged the village green cricket of Nantwich for the Stately Home venue of Lords and the MCC Centenary Test. He would be accompanied by Hornby who was to Captain the MCC team, Barlow and Pilling who along with Briggs had been selected for the England squad for the Centenary match.

The MCC Centenary match of 1887 attracted the best players throughout the land. It was to be played on the 13th, 14th, and 15th June of that year. The team sheet read as a Who's Who of the greatest cricketers playing in England at that time. Various counties had players representing England or the MCC. Gloucester were represented by Dr W G Grace, Lancashire by Mr A N Hornby, Pilling, Barlow and Johnny Briggs, Nottinghamshire by Barnes, Gunn, Flowers, Shrewsbury and Sherwin, Yorkshire Hon. M B Hawke, Bates, Hall, Rawlin and Ulyett, Surrey Mr W W Read, Lohmann and Maurice Read, Middlesex Messrs. A G Webb, J G Walker, and A E Stoddart and Kent G G Hearne. The teams lined up as follows

M.C.C.	ENGLAND
Dr WG Grace	A Shrewsbury
A N Hornby	A E Stoddart
⁰ W Barnes	R G Barlow
A J Webbe	M Read
W Gunn⁰	⁰ W W Read
G G Hearne	W Bates
J G Walker	G Ulyett
Hon. M B Hawke	L Hall
W Flowers	J Briggs
J T Rawling	G A Lohmann
+M Sherwin	+ R Pilling
⁰ Captain	+ Wicket Keeper

Just before 12.00 noon on the first day the appearance of England in the field indicated that Marylebone had won the toss and has was the practice in those days decided to bat first irrespective of the weather of the state of the pitch.

In brief the MCC made 175, W Gunn top scoring with 61. Johnny Briggs took 3 for 84. When England batted

Shrewsbury and Stoddart settled in and despite the bowling undergoing almost every conceivable connotation and the field being changed constantly they both went serenely on to amass an opening partnership of 266 runs, Shrewsbury eventually out for 152 and Stoddart for 151, England's first innings totalled 514. In MCC second knock despite 45 from Grace, a 53 from Barnes and a somewhat belated knock of 43 from Flowers they were all out for 222. England winning by an innings and 117 runs. Briggs bowling figures for the second innings were 4 for 77. Amongst the 7 wickets he took in the match were those of his Lancashire captain and friend A N Hornby and that of his long term acquaintance W G Grace. Hornby knew Briggs was bowling well and Grace had practiced with Johnny years before when he was at Hornsea, it says a lot about Briggs and his bowling that he managed to force both experienced batsmen into false strokes, the score-card for both Hornby and Grace reading c and b Briggs. Of his other five victims four were clean bowled and the other one caught.

1887 was the year of Queen Victoria's Jubilee and in the domestic game Surrey were to be crowned Champions, Lancashire won 10 matches and finished runners up to Surrey in the Championship. Frank Sugg arrived at Lancashire via Yorkshire and Derbyshire, he was a professional for both the cricket and football club at Burnley in 1885 and immediately his two years residential qualification was complete he signed for Lancashire rejecting Derbyshire. Also Lancashire recruited Joseph Eccles from local cricket and in 1887 he played every match and had the highest run aggregate in the Championship. Sugg added solidarity to Lancashire's batting and Watson and Briggs took over 100 wickets each, Briggs also scoring 800 runs to consolidate his reputation as an all-rounder. Amongst Briggs' haul of wickets that season included the following analysis

Lancashire v Cheshire	1st innings	5 for 34
Lancashire v Kent	1st innings	7 for 44
Lancashire v Nottinghamshire	2nd innings	7 for 53
Lancashire v Oxford Univ.	2nd innings	6 for 31
Lancashire v Northamptonshire	1st innings	6 for 49
Lancashire v Surrey	2nd innings	5 for 45
Lancashire v Sussex	1st innings	6 for 36

The game against Nottinghamshire at Trent Bridge in July produced a hat trick and it appears to be the last reference in a Lancashire match to a collection bring taken on the field for the bowler of a hat trick. John Auger Dixon a 26 year old medium pacer dismissed Robinson, Briggs and Yates in consecutive balls and according to the Manchester Guardian it caused "some amusement when the other members of the eleven made the collection of shillings to present Mr Dixon with a new hat", and the Sporting Chronicle wrote "if the usual custom of collecting shillings from everybody in the pavilion was rigidly observed, Mr Dixon should have enough money then for quite a splendid hat".

Lancashire had made a number of improvements to the ground and its surrounds at Old Trafford and was now regarded second only to Lords for its facilities and amenities. As part of the alterations a grand looking set of iron railings were placed on the pavilion side. Unfortunately Arthur Croome the 21 year old Gloucestershire fielder when running to catch a lofty hit from Pilling missed the ball and fell on top of the railings, a spike from the top of these new railings entered his neck about an inch below the chin, the two doctors on the field E M and W G Grace carried him to the pavilion where Dr V Royle helped to stitch the wound, thankfully the railing had miss the "vital part" and although Croome took no further part in the match he was not seriously injured.

In the Roses match at Bradford that year Yorkshire made 590 runs, Lancashire's reply was 303 and they followed on. Hornby scored 92 on the third day to save his side and the match. This match saw a Roses record of 1,220 runs for the loss of 28 wickets in a three day match. The return match at Old Trafford late in the season was critical in the outcome of the Championship and a win for Yorkshire had the effect of dislodging Lancashire from the top of the table and allowed Surrey to leap frog them and win the Championship for only the second time since 1864.

4: The Pioneering Years (1888 to 1890)

THE WINTER TOUR of 1887/88 was going to turn into a "bit of a cock up in the cricketing front". Major Wardill, Manager of the 1886 Australian tour to England, stated on departing home from that tour that "the Melbourne Club intended to invite an England team to tour Australia in the winter of 1887/88", this team being a mixture of amateur and professionals and that a number of prominent amateurs had already agreed to tour. Six months later the New South Wales Authorities asked Lillywhite, Shaw and Shrewsbury to take a tour to Australia. These three gentlemen had already managed the 1881/82 team, the 1884/85 team and the 1886/87 team to Australia. The professional trio were asked to reconsider their plans but refused to do so therefore it finished up that two tours to Australia took place that winter. G F Vernon's team would play 26 matches. Lillywhite, Shaw and Shrewsbury's team would play 25 matches and 11 chosen from both touring parties would represent England in the only test to be played that winter. The combined team comprised of seven members from the Lillywhite's team and only four from the Vernon eleven, Stoddart, W W Read, Peel and Attewell. It was not surprising that it was reported that the Melbourne Cricket Club lost 2,000 pounds on G F Vernon's tour and that Shaw and Shrewsbury lost 2,400 pounds between then on their tour. Lillywhite was unable to meet his side of the bargain, and it was the last speculative venture that the professional trio undertook together.

G. F. Vernon's party to tour Australia in 1887-88, photographed in Melbourne. Back: J. T. Rawlin, M. P. Bowden, G. F. Vernon, Sir T. C. O'Brien, J. Beaumont. Centre: A. E. Newton, W. Batees, the Hon M. B. Hawke (captain), W. Attewell, R. Peel. Front: R. Abel, W. W. Read, A. E. Stoddart.

The team taken by Shaw and Shrewsbury to Australia in
1887-88. Back: G. Brann, L. C. Docker, J. Lillywhite, J. M.
Read, A. D. Pougher. Centre: G. Ulyett, R. Pilling, C. A. Smith
(capt), A. Shrewsbury, G. A. Lohmann. Front: J. M. Preston, J.
Briggs, W. Newham. The captain, 'Round-the-Corner' Smith,
later became the famous film actor, C. Aubrey Smith.

Johnny Briggs toured as part of the Lillywhite, Shaw and
Shrewsbury's team. The following figures give some idea of
the effect he had down under if only by listing his most effec-
tive innings and bowling feats.

V	XVIII of Parramata	1st innings	9 for 33
V	XXII of Maryborough	1st innings	14 for 25
V	XXII of Gumpie	1st innings	13 for 24
V	XVIII of Queensland	2nd innings	12 for 47
V	Victoria	- 75 runs with the bat	
V	XXII of Bowrial	1st innings	14 for 20
V	XXII of Orange	1st innings	12 for 37
V	XVIII of Newcastle	- 80 runs with the bat	

V	XXII of Tamworth	1st innings	11 for 45
V	1888 Australian XI	1st innings	6 for 40
V	1888 Australian XI	2nd Innings	5 for 18
V	1888 Australian XI	- 54 runs with the bat	
V	XVIII of Canterbury	2nd innings	9 for 43 (1st match)
V	XVIII of Canterbury	2nd innings	9 for 26 (2nd match)
V	XXII of Wellington	1st innings	8 for 41

One can give a number of reasons or excuses trying to devalue these figures, the strength of the opposition, uncovered pitches, state of the pitch etc. but over a number of venues and against various opposition and the fact that Briggs was to shine solely in these matches it would be undermining Briggs skill and effort not to say that these figures are anything other than exceptional and on these figures alone Johnny Briggs is up there with the best bowlers the World has ever seen.

The solitary Test match in that tour took place on the 10th, 11th, 13th, 14th and 15th February 1888 at Sydney. This match would have been the twenty second undertaken by the Vernon team and the seventeenth of the Lillywhite, Shaw and Shrewsbury team.

Nothing seemed less like a test match than this disappointing game and perhaps it should never have been adjudged to be one. One Australian wrote "the principle matches during the past fortnight by the English teams have been divested of all importance owing to the non-representative character of the Colonial XI opposing them". England won the toss and batted, Australia started well and soon had England in trouble at 57 for 5. England however, did manage to reach 113. The match was interrupted by rain several times and when the Australians batted they were all out for what was then a record low score of 42. Lohmann 5 for 17, and Peel 5 for 18 bowled unchanged throughout the first innings. England's second innings total was slightly better than the first, reaching 137 all out, this leaving the Australians 208 runs to win. England bowled them out for 82 winning by 126 runs.

Lohmann 4 for 35 and Peel 5 for 40 doing the damage with Attewell 1 for 4 closing the innings. Briggs did not bowl in this match. In this match there was no play on Saturday and on the Monday due to heavy rain. By the last day public interest had disappeared and all test match atmosphere had gone. The G F Vernon's team returned to England after the match on 9th, 10th, and 12th March arriving at Plymouth on 28th April 1888.

The Lillywhite, Shaw and Shrewsbury party travelled to New Zealand to play three matches there. Johnny Briggs recalled an incident in a match played at Wellington, New Zealand. When an opposition team member, a Mr Mottley, happened to break his bat, he returned to the pavilion for a replacement, whilst he was in the pavilion a Maori had walked to the wicket and took his guard. Lohmann who was bowling realised at once that the man thought Mottley was out, Lohmann carried on bowling taking the wicket of the Maori c and b first ball. The Maori disconsolately walked off but George Ulyett at point shouted out to him that "he was not out and in fact that was a trial ball you may go in again", Shrewsbury agreed and he went in again. The next ball he was purposely missed at slip by Maurice Read and the next ball he hit firm in the middle of the bat, he immediately called for 2 runs, when he returned to complete the second run he found Mr Mottley standing there with a new bat, Briggs noted that "the faces of the two men were a charming study" and that "it did not take long to explain to the Maori that it was a joke and he would get another innings later". The touring team left New Zealand after the match on the 30th and 31st of March travelling on the Coptic and reaching Plymouth on 12th May 1888.

In the domestic championship Briggs had another great year capturing 187 wickets and scoring 900 runs. The City News said of him "the way in which he breaks his first ball from an impossible distance from the off and then comes a perfectly straight one as fast as Spofforth's fastest must be watched to be believed. No wonder batters give him up in despair". Some of Briggs finer performances that year was as follows

5 for 15, Lancashire v Australians
6 for 4, Lancashire v Derbyshire
6 for 13, Lancashire v Gloucestershire
6 for 18, England XI v Australians
6 for 17, Shrewsbury's XI v Australians

With regards to batting his main scores were

55 for Lancashire v Kent (Manchester)
58 for Lancashire v Oxford University
126 not out Lancashire v Sussex
60 for Lancashire v Nottinghamshire
56 for Lancashire v Kent (Canterbury)

For Lancashire he was somewhat of a solitary figure and they slipped to 5th in the table, the highlight of the summer for Lancashire was a remarkable victory over the touring Australians. This was mainly due to the Reverend J N Napier who only played two games for Lancashire one in this match and the other in a Roses match. He abandoned his flock long enough to top score with 37 in Lancashire's second innings total of 154. He took 3 for 54, and 4 for 48 in the match. The Australians only need 90 runs to win in their last innings but Napier's 4 wickets and Johnny Briggs's 5 for 15 ensured that they were all out for 66 runs, Lancashire winning by 23 runs. Before the players had time to reach the Pavilion thousands of spectators had rushed across the ground and it took Napier and Briggs several minutes to get through the ground to the dressing room, an enormous crowd assembled in front of the Pavilion and cheered for Hornby, Steele, Napier and Briggs who were obliged repeatedly to bow in acknowledgement. It was a great victory and in Napier Lancashire looked to have solved their bowling problems. The match in a way was a microcosm of Johnny Briggs cricketing fame. Everyone refers to this match as the Napier match and yet without Briggs' second innings contribution of 5 for 15, Lancashire would never have been victorious. Briggs continued all his life to produce exceptional feats of bowling, year in and year out and for twelve years taking over 100 wickets a season. But if the general cricketing public were asked to name the top ten bowlers ever to grace the test match arena, it would be surprising if Johnny Briggs was amongst them. He was an unsung hero and is the forgotten man of cricket. He was recognised later in 1888 when Wisden for the first time paid an official tribute to "six great bowlers of the year". This first list included the two touring Australians C T B Turner and J J Ferris whose toll of victims 314 and 220 were fantastic. Johnny Briggs came first on the list and his seasonal figures were

Overs	Maidens	Runs	Wickets	Average
1625.1	860	1861	187	9.95

George Lohmann of Surrey came second, Yorkshire's Bobby Peel was fourth and the Somerset Captain S M J Woods was sixth on the list.

Two other notable matches that year for Lancashire was the win in May over Oxford University. Lancashire were at one time 93 for 8, following on 110 behind. Alex Watson scored an unbeaten 22 and with the help of Barchaud and Kentfield, Lancashire set Oxford 63 runs to win. Watson took 5 for 17, and Briggs 4 for 25 ensuring Lancashire were victorious by 20 runs. The second match of interest again involved Napier in his second and last match for Lancashire, he finished off the Yorkshire innings of 80 runs with a spell of 3.2 overs, 3 maidens, nil runs, 4 wickets. One spectator asked Hornby the Lancashire Captain on the first day of the match "why he was playing that bloody parson". Hornby replied that "he was told he could bat and bowl a bit". On the final day the supporter was asked what he thought of the bloody parson now, he replied to Hornby "I reken, they ought to make him a Bishop now".

On the International side of cricket, the Australians toured England again and the first test match was held at Lords on the 16th and 17th July. The match was played on a rain effected wicket and this resulted in the lowest aggregate score for 4 innings for any test match between England and Australia, that score being 291. The match ended at 4.25pm on the second day. Turner and Ferris showed themselves to be perhaps the most destructive pair ever to visit England, but the general weakness of the Australian batting plus the lack of quality change bowlers was to prove decisive later on in the tour. Play did not begin until 3.00 pm on the first day and the Australians went for the runs before the wickets deteriorated further. They scored 116 in the first innings. This was the only innings over 62 in the match. England on the close of play on the first day were 18 for 3; the wicket was even more difficult on the second day and England were soon reduced to 22 for 7. England at one point looked like following on, having to reach 36 runs to avoid this. The margin in those days for the follow on was 80 runs, England did however total 53. When Australia batted again a second time it was farcical conditions and were soon in trouble at 18 for 7. They did however rally to reach a total of 60, this leaving England 124 to win. When Grace was out after scoring 24 of the England's score of 34 for 8, the end was not far away. England were bowled out for 62 and the Australians won by 61 runs. Briggs match figures were 25. 9. 35. 4.

In the second test at the Oval it was a different story on a different wicket, it was a hard fast wicket and the Australians were to prove no match for England on this type of wicket. Australia went from 50 for 7 at lunch to 80 all out, Briggs taking 5 for 25. England went in at 4.00 pm and made a poor start and were 53 for 4 when Abel joined Barnes at the wicket. At the close of play England had struggled to 185 for 5.

The next morning England continued to struggle and were reduced to 242 for 8, then Peel and Lohmann entertained the crowd with some spirited hitting; England reaching 317 all out, which gave England a lead of 237. Australia did make a good start of their second innings but when McDonnell went after scoring 32 of their first 34 runs the wickets fell quickly and Australia were bowled out for exactly 100 by 10 minutes to 5 on the second day, England winning by 137 runs. The figure 13 was unlucky for the Australians during this match, particularly in their first innings. The match started on the 13th of the month, 3 batsmen scored 13, one scored a double

13 (26) and the other batsmen could only score 13 between them.

The result of the rubber or series depended on the last match at Old Trafford and for the third time in the series a test match was completed within two days; in fact it was the shortest test match in which there was a result. England completing the victory before lunch at 1.55 pm on the second day. Heavy rain had fallen in Manchester for 48 hours prior to the start and the conditions seemed likely to favour the Australians, as was the case at Lords. England's batsmen again struggled at 59 for 4 and then 96 for 5, however the last wicket stand of 36 runs between Briggs and Pilling delighted the Manchester home crowd and England finally posted a total of 172, this turned out to be a good score under the conditions. Australia went in at 5.40 pm and made 32 for 2 at the close of play. Next day, Australia needed 61 more runs to avoid the follow on, Australia lost 5 more wickets for 13 runs and tumbled to 45 for 7. They recovered and looked certain to make England bat again but with 12 runs short of the follow on target Peel had Lyons caught at slip by Lohmann, Peel took 7 for 31 in the first innings. Australia's second innings began with what can only be called a startling collapse, 6 wickets going down with only 7 runs on the board. A seventh wicket stand of 48 runs by Turner and Lyon pushed the Australians total up to 70 and prevented utter failure. England won the match by an innings and 121 runs and the rubber 2 to 1.

The end of 1888 saw cricket crossing new frontiers, with the first tour to South Africa which was to include two tests between South Africa and England.

1888-89 England team prior to their departure for South Africa. Standing: B. A. F. Grieve, A. C. Skinner, A. J. Fothergill, J. M. Read, R. Abel. Seated: C. A. Smith, Major Warton (manager), Hon C. J. Coventry, J. E. P. McMaster, M. P. Bowden. In front: J. H. Roberts, H. Wood. Inset: J. Briggs, (unknown), F. Hearne.

Major R Gardner Warton who had served in South Africa was determined to take a party of English Cricketers to South Africa in the winter of 1888-89. The team he selected contained seven men who appeared regularly in first class county cricket matches during the 1888 season. The party was as follows

C A Smith (Sussex Captain)
M P Bowden (Surrey)
and Professionals
R Abel (Surrey)

J M Read (Surrey)
H Wood (Surrey)
J Briggs (Lancashire)
F Hearne (Kent)
J Fothergill (Somerset)
plus Amateurs
Hon C J Coventry
J E P McMasters
J H Roberts
B A F Grieve
A C Skinner

The Captain Charles Aubrey Smith had captained the Lillywhite, Shaw and Shrewsbury side to Australia, the previous winter, although he did not play in the test that the combined Shrewsbury and Vernon teams played. Smith captained England in the first test match in South Africa but fever prevented him from playing in the second, so he remains the only cricketer to have led England on his single appearance for them in a test match. In conjunction with his team mate Monty Bowden he was later to establish a firm of stockbrokers in South Africa and he led Transvaal to victory in the inaugural Currie Cup match. In 1896 he began to pursue an interest in the theatre and then moved to Hollywood where he won fame for his portrayals of the archetypal elderly Englishmen in such films as Lives of the Bengal Lancers, The Prisoner of Zenda and Rebecca. With Boris Karloff, he fostered cricket in California and was knighted in 1944, four years before his death for his contribution to Anglo-American relations.

The tour was scheduled for 19 matches and left England on 21st November 1888 on the Garth Castle calling at Lisbon and Madeira before arriving at Cape Town on 14th for 4 at lunch but were eventually all out for 129, the match was all over by 3.30 pm on the second day England losing just two wickets on their way to reaching the 67 runs required to win the match. England won by 8 wickets.

The second test at Cape Town was remarkable and Briggs was said to be in an 'unplayable class'. For this test Bowden had replaced the ailing Smith, Bowden was the only amateur in the side with sufficient first class experience and at age 22 years and 144 days remains the youngest player to have captained England. Later that year he was to track North with the Pioneer Column of Cecil Rhodes and led an adventurous life in primitive conditions for more than two years. In February 1892 he fell from a cart and died in Umtali Hospital which in fact was little more than a glorified mud hut, a man with a revolver stood guard over the body to protect it from marauding lions. Monty Bowden England's youngest captain was buried in a coffin made from whisky crates.

In the match itself England batted first with Johnny Briggs going in at the fall of the first wicket, the move proving to be unsuccessful as he only scored six runs, Abel however the Surrey opener was to carry on and make 120 scoring the first 100 in a test match between England and South Africa. England made 212 with the help of a fine 59 from H Wood the wicket keeper. Before stumps were drawn that evening South Africa had lost Innes LBW to Fothergill and Briggs had sent down a solitary maiden.

Next morning was to be one of the most sensational mornings of cricket of all time with Briggs producing probably the most destructive pre-lunch spell of bowling in the history of first class cricket. On the morning of the second day South Africa resumed their innings on their overnight total of 2 for 1, the first innings then collapsed and they were all out for a meagre 47. Tancred with 26 not out becoming the first batsman to carry his bat through a complete test innings. Johnny Briggs had taken 7 of the 9 wickets that fell that morning for 17 runs in 8.1 overs.

South Africa followed on but faired even more disastrously when they returned to bat a second time, for when lunch came they were reduced to 36 for 7. Briggs taking 5 of the 7 for 9 runs in 13 overs. During the mornings play Briggs had taken 12 wickets for 26 runs in 31.1 overs of which 15 were maidens. Eleven of the 12 wickets Briggs took were clean bowled and the other LBW. All twelve were therefore taken without the help of a fielder. Briggs had incredible match figures of 15 wickets for 28 runs.

Other notable figures on the tour for Briggs were as follows

9 for 52 v XXII of Western Province 1st innings
14 for 84 v XXII of Western Province 2nd innings
16 for 94 v XXII of Eastern District 1st innings
12 for 59 v XXII of Eastern District 2nd innings
14 for 55 v XV of Natal
8 for 72 v XVIII of Kimberley
12 for 36 v XXII of Midland District 1st innings
9 for 11 v XXII of Midland District 2nd innings

It is amazing to record that Briggs almost unbelievable wicket per match ratio and runs per wicket on the tour. In fact he took 290 wickets at an average of 5.62 runs per wicket in the 19 match tour.

A South African newspaper reported about Johnny that "a characteristic feature of Briggs in the field is his happy go lucky style. He is undoubtedly one of the most popular professional cricketers in England and the reason is obvious, he is a clever dissembler. Up to all kinds of antics and tricks, he raises many a laugh in trying to get rid of a batsman...whilst batting he jumps in and out of his ground, strikes comical attitudes and generally acts as if he were one fourth part a clown. These antics of course would not be tolerated in a cricketer of mediocre ability, but Briggs can take liberties which would not be permitted if attempted by another man. Besides when cricket is reduced to an absolute science it is apt to become monotonous to all but enthusiasts and at such times the comicalities which the crack professional indulges in are much appreciated by the crowd".

THE JONNIBEE. This funny little chap cooms from Manchester and cracks jokes like a nut. He can roll hisself up into a ball and run all over the place like a squirl and is allways up to lots of anticks. He got spots on him, but you can't nick any off of him.

The only down side of the whole tour as far as Briggs was concerned is that he contacted sun stroke and it was about this time his epileptic fits became more frequent. Mr Hornby in later years attributed Johnny's death to this, but that was eleven years later that Johnny died and the fits became stronger and more regular, so it was by no means certain that sun stroke did contribute to Johnny's eventual demise.

The side sailed back to England on the Garth Castle again arriving on the 16th April 1889. C A Smith and M P Bowden remained behind in South Africa.

The Annual meeting of the MCC was held on 1st May 1889 in the Pavilion of the Lords Cricket ground. The committee were to recommend to the meeting that a number of alterations should be made to the rules of the game.

- Firstly, to substitute 5 ball overs for 4.
- Secondly, that a bowler may change ends as often as he likes but cannot bowl 2 overs in succession
- Thirdly, on the last day of a match and in a one day match at any time the in-side may declare their innings at an end.

All counties were in favour of the alterations with the exception of Surrey who disapproved altogether and Nottinghamshire who were divided as to the question of the number of balls in an over. In the end the proposed alterations were all carried unanimously. There was no visiting team playing in England in 1889 so all eyes were on the Championship.

In 1888, Charles Pardon (The Editor of Wisden) had invented a new system of deciding the championship and this was to be used for the first time in the 1889 season. Basically it was very simple, in fact too simple. One point was to be awarded for a win and half a point for a draw.

The Lancashire committee granted Richard Pilling the Lancashire wicket keeper a Benefit in 1888. Pilling was always a delicate creature, almost fragile and was constantly ill during the season. He accompanied the Lancashire team to Dublin in June, in the hope of regaining his health. Unfortunately Pilling experienced a severe attack of pleurisy and was still unwell when the team returned to Manchester. He was left out of the team to play Oxford University so that he might recover enough to play the important forthcoming matches against Nottinghamshire and Surrey.

Although he was weak he played in the defeat at Nottinghamshire and in the Victory over Surrey, by the time of his Benefit match Pilling was feeling much better but missed the match North v South at Old Trafford due to an injured hand. It was a measure of the high regard in which Pilling was held that no other matches were played that weekend in July, in order that the counties could send their best players to the match. The match was watched by 30,000 people and it produced a record 1,500 pound for the wicket keeper.

1889 was an interesting season and one of the finest Roses matches of all time was played out at Huddersfield (Fartown) in the summer of that year. Lancashire batted first in the match Hornby and Eccles facing Ulyett and Peel, the Yorkshire bowlers, the contrasting style of these two forming an ideal opening attack. Five wickets fell in the first hour, Ulyett claiming three and Peel two, it was then that Briggs stemmed the tide. "Not by dour defence but gay attack". Once Sugg was next out two more wickets fell quickly but Briggs kept up the fight and when Briggs went, Watson took a leaf out of Briggs book and hit out to score a couple of boundaries. When Pilling was caught behind the Lancashire innings was completed with a score of 81 on the board. Yorkshire start was almost as bad as Lancashire's. Hall had his middle stump uprooted, Lee then came in with a single run on the board and played one of his finest innings, Lee did see however Wade go quickly and then Peel, who "after a huge hit or two returned the ball red hot to Briggs, the little man grasped it affectionately to his bosom as if it had been no more than an orange, and three wickets were down". Lee hit out at almost every ball and Lord Hawkes was equally aggressive, Lord Hawkes innings included a six over square leg. In those days a six had to go completely out of the ground, not just over the boundary ropes. He went on to make an unbeaten 52 and Yorkshire 160.

When Lancashire batted for the second time they had tumbled to 22 for 4 at the close of play on the first day. Mold went early doors on the second day and Lancashire stood at 27 for 5, still needing over 50 to save an innings defeat. It was then that Briggs entered the fray. "Gay, impudent, as resilient as a rubber ball, a little skip jack of a man". He immediately began to hit out and the field that had been crowding him spread out. Briggs was in the mood when he was almost impossible to contain, and the only way for Yorkshire to break the stand between him and Ward was to remove Ward. Briggs grew more and more "daring in his driving", and "daintily impertinent in his cutting and placing". Briggs kept up his dashing cavalier style tactics and by the time he was caught behind, he had added 50 priceless runs to the score. There was then some hard hitting from Paul, Baker and Watson and by the close of the innings, Lancashire had totalled 153 and Yorkshire had to bat again but only to score 75 runs to achieve a noticeable victory over the old enemy.

Yorkshire soon realised that this was not going to be a formality. Mold got rid of Hull, Wade, Lee and Ulyett in quick succession and the score was then 9 runs for 4 wickets. Yorkshire had their backs to the wall but even at 24 for 6 all was not lost. Peel and Wainwright played intelligently but then Peel turning sharply for a second run slipped and fell on his face, it was said that you could see him trying to regain his ground "trying to drag the crease towards him", but Pilling had whipped the bails off - 38 for 7. Yorkshire's score moved slowly but surely forward, the eighth wicket adding 25 runs, the total now standing at 63. The innings then took on a single figure count down, Yorkshire scoring single by single. Four runs were needed when Mold bowled Whitehead neck and crop. The last man in was Middlebrook and it is fair to say the Number eleven was not one of nature's master batsman. Whether he ever saw the three balls he faced is very doubtful, the first two whizzing over his bails.

The third just touched the edge of his bat and was caught by Hornby at silly point.

Yorkshire had lost by three runs.

Lancashire tied with Surrey and Nottingham at the top of the Championship in 1889 and it was largely thanks to their main three bowlers Briggs, Mold and Watson. The Lancashire bowlers occupied three of the four top places in the bowling averages for that year.

	Overs	Maidens	Runs	Wickets	Average
Attewell (Notts)	1364.2	673	1635.	149	10.97
Briggs (Lancs)	1040.3	447	1646	140	11.75
Mold (Lancs)	679	262	1207	102	11.85
Watson (Lancs)	850.3.	438	1139.	90	12.65

By the 8th August, Nottinghamshire had won eight and lost one, Surrey won seven and lost two and Lancashire won seven and lost three. Rain resulted in a further draw for all three counties, though Lancashire did have victories over Sussex and critically Surrey. Near the end of the season Lancashire and Surrey had completed all their matches but Nottinghamshire had still one game to play, all three counties had ten and a half

December, in fact the tour was a joint enterprise between Major Warton and Sir Donald Currie who owned the Garth Castle. Sir Donald was the founder of the Castle line (later to become the Union Castle) and also founded the Currie Cup in South Africa which is the equivalent of the County Championship in England or Sheffield Shield in Australia.

Johnny Briggs had a number of amazing analysis whilst on this tour, the most notable will be outlined later, but the matches between the XXII of Cape Mounted Rifles, Kingwilliamstown on 23rd to 25th February and the two tests at Port Elizabeth on the 12th and 13th March and Cape Town on 25th and 26th March need further examination and detailing. In the match against the XXII of Cape Mounted Rifles, Briggs first innings figures were described as being "almost a miracle" he actually took 15 wickets for 4 runs in the first innings and when the soldiers batted a second time he captured 12 of their wickets for 19 runs, so his total match analysis or figures were 27 wickets for 23 runs in the match.

In the first test which is now regarded as the first official test match between the Countries, the South African team with the exception of the absent Theunissen of Cape Town was the strongest team that could be formed and 3,000 people were present to see the start of the game. The South Africans were to be no match for the tourists, Briggs taking the first two wickets both bowled without a run on the board. Tancred with 29 on the board and Dunell the South African Captain with 26 not out, were the main contributors to the South African total of 84. Briggs taking 4 for 39. When England batted they found themselves in trouble at 87 for 8 but recovered somewhat to make a final score of 148 all out, thanks to a 14 not out be Grieve and a timely 32 by Fotheringill. South Africa did better in their second innings when they were 67 points and were leading the Championship. Nottinghamshire made a complete mess of their last match at Kent losing by 4 wickets. Therefore to the embarrassment of Mr Pardon and his new scoring system the Championship ended in a triple tie. The cricketing press including the Lillywhite's Annual (Wisden and Pardon's main rival) attacked the system and suggested that Nottinghamshire deserved first place and because Lancashire had defeated Surrey both home and away should be second. In the end a triple tie stood but they suggested that the whole point system should be reviewed urgently. A meeting of the County Secretaries had completed this task by the beginning of the 1890 season.

5: The Departing and Resurgent Years
(1890 to 1892)

THE CRICKET COUNCIL had for the first time in 1890 recognised the existence of the competition amongst the Counties and it was therefore the first year of the official County Championship. The Inaugural match taking place on the 12th to 14th May when Gloucester entertained Yorkshire at Bristol.

The new scoring system involved gaining one point for a win and also deducting one point for a loss, drawn matches would be completely ignored. So for example if you had played ten matches, won six, lost two and drawn two, your total points at that time of the season would be four.

The 50s

The 60s

The 70s

The 80s

The 90s

IN THE OLD DAYS CRICKETERS WERE PICTURESQUE PERSONALITIES

The game grows up. (Drawing by "RIP!")

In 1890 the Australians visited England under the management of H F Boyle of Victoria and the captaincy of W L Murdock. On the third match of this tour they played a Mr W H Laverton XI at Westbury near Leighton, Wiltshire on the 15th, 16th, and 17th May. Mr Laverton's XI beating the touring Australians by 67 runs, Johnny Briggs taking 7 for 33 in the first innings and 4 for 59 in the second. However an incident off the field caused some amusement amongst the players. Johnny Briggs had joined a small rook shooting party. Everybody concerned with the shoot enjoyed it immensely, and when Johnny got back to the ground the next day he boasted about his shooting abilities. When lunch was being taken the smile on Johnny's face soon disappeared as a policeman served him with a summons for shooting without a licence. What made matters worse was that he had to return in person to answer the summons on the very day that the Lancashire match against Gloucestershire was due to start. He was "considerably flustered" and was more than relieved when he found out the truth of the matter for as the report of the incident states "the summons was only fictitious bit of writing" and Briggs had been "completely taken in", but he found consolation while "trembling under the outstretched and threatening arm of the law" that members of the team had offered to post bail and if the worst had come to the worst he was not going to be short of friends.

In the rain affected match against Sussex, Lancashire invoked one of the new rules that had been passed on 1st May the previous year, that of declaring on the last day of a match. There was no play on the first day at Old Trafford in this game due to rain and play did not commence until after lunch on the second. Johnny Briggs (129 not out) and Albert Ward then put together a stand of 215, Lancashire's score standing at 246 for 2 at the close of play. There was no play again on the morning of the third and last day, play resuming at 2.15pm. It was then Arthur Kemble the stand-in wicket keeper in the absence of the ill Pilling, who was captaining the side, chose to declare. Alex Watson and Briggs then took control of the match with figures of 5 for 7 and 4 for 25 respectively. Sussex being bowled out for 35 runs in an hour and 40 mins. The Sussex second innings lasted for only an hour by which time Watson (4 for 6) and Briggs (5 for 16) had dismissed Sussex for 24. Briggs' 5 wickets coming in a 7 ball stint. The City News pointed out that the match had no parallel, Lancashire's two wickets having beaten Sussex 20, Lancashire winning by an innings and 187 runs.

Lancashire had the upper hand in the rain affected match against Yorkshire, Lancashire had scored 161 runs (Briggs 52) in the first innings and when Yorkshire batted, Mold was in superb form with the ball and took 8 for 32 when Yorkshire totalled 88. In Lancashire's second knock Briggs hit another half century (54) and backed up by Paul, Lancashire reached 187 leaving Yorkshire to get 261 for Victory, they lost two wickets for two runs in the remaining overs prior to close of play. Rain washed out the last day. Unfortunately towards the finish of the second day Briggs strained himself in the field and could not play for the next month, because of the injuries he received. This injury plus the absence of Pilling reduced Lancashire's prowess in the field considerably. Although Briggs missed a month of the season he still took 86 wickets for Lancashire and 158 wickets in total that season.

With regards to Pilling the Lancashire committee were concerned enough about his welfare that they paid for him to go to Australia in an attempt to cure his illness, this action showing what regard he was held in at Old Trafford.

Pilling wrote to the committee before the voyage

"I cannot leave England without writing to thank you from the bottom of my heart for the kindness you have always shown to me and particularly in my long illness. I beg also to thank you most sincerely for the handsome sum (150 pounds) you have so generously voted, towards my trip to Australia. I hope that I may be benefited by the trip and that on my return I will be able to take my place once more in the team. With much respect I remain, Gentlemen, Your Grateful and Obedient Servant. (Signed) R Pilling".

On a brighter side 1890 saw the arrival of Archie MacLaren who had captained Harrow that year in the drawn match against Eton at Lords, scoring 76 of his team's total of 133. The City News reported that Lancashire had a promising recruit in the person of Mr A C MacLaren the son of James MacLaren, the Lancashire treasurer.

He made his debut against Sussex at Brighton in May of that year. After Sussex had made 86 the Lancashire's score stood at 9 for 2 when he went in and despite the poor pitch made 108 in 130 minutes and was reported that "he did not give a ghost of a chance and his innings throughout was a most dashing display". The City News also stated "the importance to Lancashire of such a recruit who has all his life before him and who in the ordinary course of things would go on improving, cannot be overestimated". How right this statement turned out to be. Lancashire finished second in the Championship to Surrey, the full table using the new scoring scheme was as follows

	Played	Won.	Lost.	Drawn	Points
1. Surrey	14	9	3	2	6
2. Lancashire	14	7	3	4	4
3. = Kent	14	6	3	5	3
3. = Yorkshire	14	6	3	5	3
5. Nottinghamshire	14	5	5	4	0
6. Gloucestershire	14	5	6	3	-1
7. Middlesex	12	3	8	1	-5
8. Sussex	12	1	11	0	-10

On the International front the visiting Australians had a programme of 39 matches starting on the 8th May and finishing on 20th September. The first test match at Lords beginning on 21st July was to be their twenty second match of the tour.

England made two changes to the originally selected team for this match J M Read and Barnes taking the place of Stoddart and Briggs. Briggs having picked up a strain in the Yorkshire match and therefore could not play. Stoddart placed county before Country and played for Middlesex instead of England. Rain had again fallen in what was to be a wet summer and the wicket and the scores improved throughout the game. It was a low key match Australia batting first after winning the toss and making 132 after Lyons and Turner had reached 66 before the fall of the first wicket.

England scored 173 (after being reduced to 20 for 4), thanks to a splendid 74 from "Happy Jack" Ulyett, so called because of his habit of always whistling. In the second Australian innings Barrett moved up the order to open with Turner and when Turner went Lyons scored a quick 33 in 25 minutes, Barrett watched people come and go, becoming the first player to carry his bat in a completed innings in a test match between England and Australia. His contribution was 67 in his team's total of 176. England made the 137 runs needed for victory with a loss of 3 wickets. W G Grace being 75 not out at the end. It was the first time that no byes had been conceded in a test match.

The second test was held at the Oval on the 11th and 12 August, again Briggs was unavailable and again Stoddart preferred to play for Middlesex against Yorkshire.

Peel and Ulyett also preferred to play for Yorkshire in the same match rather than to play in the test at the Oval. These withdrawals resulted in three new players making their debut for England, Cranston, Sharpe and Martin. Martin was to take 6 for 50 in the first Australian innings and 6 for 52 in the second making him the first play to take 12 wickets on his debut.

Again the wicket had been adversely affected by rain over-night and after winning the toss Murdock the Australian captain made what was to prove to be an unwise decision; that was to bat first. Showers fell during the innings and the wicket deteriorated progressively. Australia made 92 in their first knock, England 8 more at 100. When Australia returned to the crease they fared little better amassing 102 runs, this left England to get 95 for Victory. With the pitch deteriorating by the hour this was to be no easy task. When Grace was dropped of the first ball thus avoiding getting a pair of "spectacles" England's chance of winning increased. England although at one time comfortable, at 82 for 4 collapsed to 93 for 8, MacGregor England's wicket keeper later recalled the match and its finish. He stated "there was 11 to get when I went in and things seemed to be going alright when a wicket fell. It was Sharpe's turn to bat and there was still two runs to get. We had a little talk and agreed to run if the ball went to Lyons who was fielding at third man just far enough away to make a run possible. However as it happened we either forgot our arrangement of misunderstood each other, for the ball went straight to Barrett at cover point and Sharpe and I met half way down the wicket just as he fielded the ball, there seemed little chance of escape, but Barrett to our great relief chucked the ball over the head of Ferris and we ran two for an over throw and the match was won", The third test match was to held at Old Trafford on the 25th, 26th and 27th August. Because it rained on all of those three days, the match was abandoned without a ball being bowled.

After Hornby probably Barlow was the one who had influenced Briggs more than any other Lancashire cricketer. But Briggs sole mates and companions for years and groomsman at his wedding in 1885 were Barlow, Pilling and Watson. Both Barlow and Pilling would be departing in different ways during 1891.

It was with interest that Briggs looked forward to the return of Pilling from his convalescing journey to Australia. Pilling's health had improved during his journey but "a relapse took place and dropsy intervened". Pilling accompanied by Mr James Benton of Old Trafford left Australia for home early, sailing from Sydney on the 2nd February 1891. "Mr Benton was afraid the end was approaching and wanted to get him home to breathe his last". Pilling's widow later stated that "it was a great comfort to me to be near him and administer to his sufferings". When he was dying Pilling told his wife that he had "left her amply provided for and the income from his sports outfitting business would be sufficient to keep her and their three children". Pilling arrived back in Manchester on the 23rd March and passed away on the 29th of that month with Consumption.

Pilling was in partnership with Watson in his sports outfitting business. Watson bought Mrs Pilling out soon after her husband's death, paying 50 pounds for her husband's name, Mrs Pilling protested and the solicitors argued in the newspaper columns about the deal and she soon went into business with Johnny Briggs.

The business was then to be called *Pilling and Briggs*.

It was not uncommon for Cricketers in those days to set up in business in either a sports outfitters shop, a pub, or a tobacconist shop, indeed Barlow himself ran a sports outfitters shop before becoming groundsman at Old Trafford on his retirement, he also in later years was to become a County and Test match umpire.

The end of Barlow's career in 1891 was a sad affair he was asked by the Lancashire committee to stand down from the Essex match in August of that year.

The match was a second class match and would not count in the championship and the committee thought that there were a number of young players who deserved a trial. Barlow's reply was to the fact that if he did not play in this match he would not play again. At the next Annual General meeting the match committee decided that Barlow should not play whether he liked it or not, an amendment was proposed to the statement to be sent to Barlow that the Club "recognised the valuable service of Barlow and regretted the severance of his connection with the team". However this amendment was defeated at the meeting by 200 votes to 4. Barlow was never to play again in a first class match. Hornby chose him to go on the Southern tour, starting at Gravesend on 17th August but the committee over-ruled him. Barlow did play once more in the following year against Cheshire, a minor county, and only then at the request of Hornby who wrote to Sam Squires:

"Dear Sam

I hope you will play Barlow against Cheshire now do to please me. Write me Lochnivar, Sutherlandshire. Yours as ever."

Back came the following reply:

"My Dear Hornby

... solely out of deference to your personal desire he will be asked to play. At the same time the committee wish you to understand that they have not in any way altered their opinion as to Barlow's fitness to take part in a First Eleven of Lancashire."

W G Grace was to remark that "Barlow was left out of the Lancashire team long before he had lost his form". Briggs had lost two of his long term colleagues in a matter of months.

In the Championship the eight founder members were joined by Somerset for the first time in 1891. For Lancashire that season Mold was in splendid form and headed the bowling averages with 129 wickets, costing 12.62 runs each. Johnny Briggs provided Mold with great support taking 89 wickets in 15 first class matches, although it was noted that "Lancashire suffered in 1891 because illness limited the appearance and performance of the redoubtable Briggs". Despite this Briggs was to post the following figures.

Lancashire v Yorkshire	6 for 76
Lancashire v Yorkshire	8 for 46
Lancashire v Kent	5 for 35
Lancashire v Surrey	8 for 58
Lancashire v Sussex	8 for 54
Lancashire v Sussex	5 for 30
Lancashire v MCC	5 for 36

When playing at Scarborough for the North v South

that season Briggs completed the hat-trick by dismissing W L Murdock, E M Hadow and J J Ferris in successive balls. During the season Briggs took 153 wickets at an average of 11 runs per wicket.

Lancashire finished second again to Surrey in the Championship that year.

The winter tour to Australia was to all intense and purposes, somewhat a gamble, following on from the disastrous dual tour of 1887-1888. Cricket had been losing its popularity in Australia and squabbles between the Melbourne and Sydney clubs did not help this cause whatsoever. Lord Sheffield, the great patron of Sussex cricket; stated that he would take the responsibility and organise the tour but finance would only be made available if W G Grace agreed to captain the side. When he agreed the gamble looked a better bet Both Shrewsbury and Gunn refused the terms offered by Lord Sheffield but there were no other refusals. The team that went to Australia was therefore the following

W G Grace (Gloucestershire)
O G Radcliffe (Gloucestershire)
A E Stoddart (Middlesex)
G MacGregor (Cambridge University)
H Philipson (Northumberland)
And the professionals were
G A Lohmann (Surrey)
R Abel (Surrey)
J M Read (Surrey)
J W Sharpe (Surrey)
W Attewell (Nottinghamshire)
R Peel (Yorkshire)
J Briggs (Lancashire)
G Bean (Sussex)

Alfred Shaw was recruited to manage the team and the tour. The team played matches in Malta and Colombo on the outward journey. The first match in Adelaide was scheduled to begin on 20th November 1891

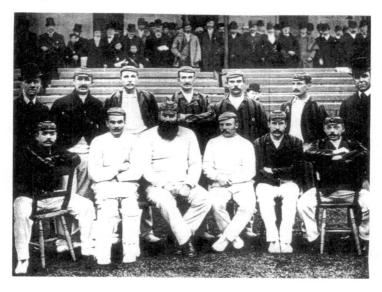

Lord Sheffield's England party for the 1891-92 tour of Australia. Back row: Carpenter (umpire), Attewell, Lohmann, M. Read, Bean, Sharpe, Thoms (umpire). Front: Briggs, MacGregor, Grace, Peel, Stoddart, Abel.

After the match in Colombo the team went out on the town before returning to their boat about 12 midnight. Briggs was in charge of getting all the partying members safely back on board their ship. Unfortunately the combination of the dark and the drink, poor Johnny took them onto a boat which was just starting out for China. The party realised their mistake just in time.

Gregor MacGregor the England wicket keeper, when asked

if he found the long journey's tedious replied "not at all there was always something or other going on, on one occasion we had a Christy Minstrel entertainment and the rehearsals were always productions of great deal of fun. Briggs of course was one of the corner men and Grace was to be Mr Johnson with his face blacked and his beard nicely powdered".

Among other things Briggs had to tell Mr Johnson a story about a dog and to understand this story; it has to be realised that in 1891 a curr was another name for a mongrel, a mutt or a stray. MacGregor continued that "Briggs had to tell Johnson a yarn about his poor little dog which had been run over in the Strand". This was to give Mr Johnson the opportunity of making the fine old crusted remark "how did it occur?" to which Briggs had to answer, "it isn't any more a curr than you are". But no matter how carefully he was coached W G Grace invariably used to ask with great solemnity "how did it happen?" which of course upset matters altogether. On the eventful evening when the actual performance took place everybody was on tiptoes of expectation to see how Briggs would get out of the usual difficulty, but Mr Johnson was equal to the occasion and brought the house down by the ease in which he enquired "how it occurred".

The England party were confident after their wins over Australia in England and after winning the first two matches that confidence seemed to be well founded. The first test match at Melbourne on New Year's day 1892. This was the first test match to adopt a six ball over format. Australia batted with "steadiness rather than brilliance", with Bannerman making 45 runs in 195 minutes in the first innings and 41 in 240 minutes in the second it was never going to be a free scoring match. Nevertheless the Australians made a more than useful 240 runs, when England batted they had made 84 runs before the fall of the first wicket. Grace made 50, Bean 50 and Briggs a handy 41 runs in England's first innings total of 264, a lead of 24. When Grace was batting he was so discomforted by the closeness of the field he asked Blackham the Australian captain and wicket keeper "if he wanted a funeral in his team". Grace did not make himself popular with the home supporters when he refused the limping Australian batsman Moses a runner in their first innings and were even less pleased with him when he objected to the substitute fielder Hutton when he was about to replace the injured McLeod. Grace was reported to ask Blackham concerning Hutton "is he a better fielder than McLeod?" Blackham replied "yes he is", to which Grace responded "then get someone else". Donnan became the second substitute fielder.

In the Australian second knock Lyons top scored with 51 but seven other batsmen reached double figures in the combined total of 236. England were then set to score a very gettable score of 213, this would be the lowest total of the match. At 60 without loss in their second innings England looked to be in with a good chance, at 98 for 7, all hope had gone, they did manage to reach 158 but Australia had won by 54 runs.

At the second test at Sydney at the end of January, Australia won the toss and batted first and when Lyons hit Briggs to the score board and then lifted Lohmann into the ladies pavilion it was obvious that the Australians were in an aggressive mood.

However they collapsed and were all out for 145, Lohmann taking 8 for 58 in 43.2 overs. England started well in their innings again reaching 50 without loss, Abel batted for 5 hours and 24 minutes making 132 and carrying his bat throughout the innings. Johnny Briggs was second top scorer with 28 in England's total of 307 giving them a lead of 162. When Australia batted a second time, starting late on the second day they lost Trott when the score was one and with Moses unable to bat England were well in control of the game. On the third day Bannerman again held up one end scoring 67 runs in the complete days play, nevertheless Australia did reach 263 for 3 placing them 101 runs in front by the close of play.

At the start of the fourth days play Australia added 36 runs without loss before rain stopped play. The uncovered wicket was drenched. Australia went on to reach 390 for 6 before Briggs came on to bowl and ended their innings when he bowled Giffen had Callaway caught by Grace off the next delivery and Blackham LBW the next.

Thus finishing the innings with a "hat" trick. England went in to bat at the end of the fourth day and were quickly reduced to 11 for 3 by stumps. Unusually Grace came in for some criticism for not sending in tail-enders at this point of play. Despite a fine 69 from Stoddart England were bowled out for 157, Australia winning by 72 runs and leading the series 2 nil with one to play.

Briggs remains the only player to score a century and take a "hat" trick in test matches what is more he did it against Australia in Australia.

With the series lost the last test had only academic interest. England replaced MacGregor with Philipson and Australia brought in Gregory and Donnan for Moses (injured) and Callaway. England made a good start the second wicket falling at 121.

Stoddart batted for 230 minutes to make 134, England progressing to 313 for 4 at stumps at the end of the first day.

Peel (83) and Briggs (39) batted in entertaining fashion the following morning and England posted a score of 499. At the end of the innings rain had begun to fall and at start of play on the third day the pitch was in a dreadful state. Briggs was practically unplayable on such a pitch and he took 6 for 49 in Australians first innings of 100 and 6 for 87 in the second when Australia reached 169. Briggs therefore had match figures of 12 for 136 and England had won by an innings and 230 runs.

Briggs other notable figures on the tour were

91 with a bat	v	South Australia
5 for 10	v	New South Wales
12 for 38	v	XX of Cumberland
13 for 29	v	XXII of Camden
12 for 46	v	XXIV of Bowral
12 for 41	v	XXIV of Bowral
13 for 29	v	XXII of Baimsdale
5 for 33	v	Victoria
74 with a bat	v	XVIII of North Tasmania

Originally the England's teams expenses were estimated at £11,000 but they finished up at £16,000 with the receipts failing to recover the costs by £2,700. Lord Sheffield considering this to be a fair price to pay for the tour. The effect of the tour on Australian cricket "was dramatic" according to the Australian newspaper, which said "it was like an electric current". Tom Horan in his article the "International Match" published in the same paper on 9th January 1892 wrote "those who were under the impression that the visit of Lord Sheffield's team would not be beneficial to Australian cricket have changed their minds, and it is now their concurrent testimony of all that the visit has caused a cricket revival which has surpassed even the more sanguine anticipations of those who viewed the tour favourably when it was first proposed".

Inter state cricket was further stimulated that year by the creation of the Sheffield Shield competition. Lord Sheffield on departing back to England left a farewell present on £150 to be used as thought best by the Australian cricket council. At a meeting on 13th September 1892 after long a detailed discussion, the vote was 6 to 5 in favour of creating the Sheffield Shield, the Chairman did not vote. After further discussions concerning the details of the trophy it was decided that it should consist of a shield bearing the Arms of Australia and the Earls of Sheffield. The Australian Cricket Councils Annual General Meeting held on 28th December 1893 at the Vienna Cafe, Melbourne, awarded the contract to Philip Blashki, a jeweller of Bourke Street, Melbourne. The Sheffield Shield trophy was finally completed on the 14th July 1894 and since that time has been the premier cricketing trophy in Australia.

There was also a smaller winter tour in 1891-92 to South Africa, this 20 match tour was led by W W Read and among its members were two ex-Australian test cricketers who had recently emigrated to England. The ex-captain of Australia W L Murdock who was then playing for Sussex and the fast bowler J J Ferris who was engaged by Gloucestershire.

On the domestic front at Lancashire, Hornby had reconsidered his decision to retire as captain but still only played four championship games that season leaving Crossfield to lead the side in the remaining matches. It was to turn out to be one of the poorest seasons Lancashire were to have for a number of years only finishing fourth in the championship. Surrey winning the trophy for the fifth consecutive year followed by Nottinghamshire and Somerset. Lancashire's batting looked strong on paper but they collapsed too often. Crossfield said "I cannot account for it, nor can anyone else. I believe we are strong in batting than we have ever been and twice have made over 400 over this year and twice of 300. But sometimes for no particular reason we go to pieces". Lancashire also lost their first Roses match in four years but did make Yorkshire struggle to get the 61 runs needed for victory in their second innings, they were 33 for 6 at one stage but then did not lose another wicket.

Punctuality in the starting, finishing of the games and the length of the intervals were no way as rigidly enforced as they are today, and no allowance was made for adding on time at the end of the first two days play if there was a chance of a result.

If the end of a game was close, the captains could agree to keep going instead of returning the following morning to complete the fixture.

Concerning the Lancashire match against Middlesex at Old Trafford the Manchester Courier pointed out the need for punctuality in matches when it said "punctuality is equally the soul of cricket as it is in business". It said that 15 minutes were lost at the start of the first day and 10 minutes on the second. Middlesex needed 227 for victory in this match and were reduced to 102 for 8 at the end of the second day.

Alex Webbe the Middlesex captain refused to continue playing and when rain settled in on the last day of the match, Middlesex escaped with a draw. Webbe's action though strictly within his rights was considered sharp practice. Webbe was not alone in refusing to continue a game. Kent, in the previous match against Lancashire made them go back for a third day at Tonbridge when they had no chance of winning the game.

Lancashire scored 484 and Kent had replied with 47 for 2, which it rained heavily for two and a half hours. Mold and Briggs then took 16 wickets for 95 runs in 85 minutes. Kent reached the close of play still needing 345 runs to avoid an innings defeat with only two wickets left. Frank Marchant the Kent captain refused to continue but play did start early the following day so that the Lancashire team could get their 3.00 pm train from St Pancras station. The game was over within 20 minutes Mold taking 9 for 29.

Another opportunity to finish a game was the Somerset match at Old Trafford in August. The first day was washed out completely and the match was decided on the following day. Somerset batted first and reached 60 for 2, but then collapsed to 88 all out. Briggs bowling throughout the innings and taking 7 for 62. Lancashire made 116 in their first knock. Somerset fared even worse when they returned to the crease making only a mere 58 runs, Briggs again doing the damage with 5 for 21. By that time it was 6.15 pm and Lancashire needed only 31 runs to win. Hewett the Somerset captain "saw that defeat was inevitable and faced it in a manly fashion instead of playing for a draw". He agreed to continue playing until the game was completed and Lancashire secured victory by 8 wickets before 7.00 pm.

Lancashire extracted sweet revenge for the defeat in Yorkshire winning the return fixture by an innings and 83 runs. Johnny Briggs had the sort of match cricketers only dream about. He scored 115 runs with the bat then bowled unchanged throughout Yorkshire's first innings taking 8 wickets for 113 runs in just over 50 overs and with Watson as his accomplish again demolished the Yorkshire batting in the second innings.

Despite any winter tour or hard season Johnny Briggs would always find time to play in his father's annual benefit match at the end of the season at Widnes. In fact many famous cricketers would take part in James Briggs benefits throughout the years a number attending at Johnny's personal request. The cricketers that played at the Lowerhouse Lane Ground included the following

Shrewsbury, Hornby, Steel, Bar1ow, Pilling, Sugg, Mold, Sharpe, Mar1ow, Jo Briggs, Burns, Watson, Tinsley, Paul, Roder, Rowley, Robinson and Ward.

Johnny Briggs was noted for his happy go lucky disposition, but in addition to this as the Cricket Weekly Record noted "he was exceedingly good natured and kind hearted" I adding somewhat poignantly "like most humorists he had his serious side for he had many worries and troubles".

In the October of 1892 Lord Hawke captained a team of amateurs to Ceylon and India but there was no winter tour to Australia that year. The Australians were however to send a party to England for a 36 match tour in the summer of 1893.

6: The Record Years
(1893 to 1895)

THE AUSTRALIAN TOURING team of 1893 had a strong batting line up but the bowling was comparatively weak and it was not helped by the general slovenliness in the field which in the end turned out to be an epidemic of dropped catches.

The first test at Lords on 17th, 18th, and 19th July was the twenty first match of the tour and England included the debutants F S Jackson, W H Lockwood and Briggs' Lancashire colleague A Mold. Briggs did not take part in this match. Stoddart captained the team in the place of the absent Grace, his opposite number being Blackham whose captaincy came in for considerable criticism during the tour and he failed to get the best out of his team all tour.

England batted first and lost two early wickets at 29 and 31, but a stand of 137 in 105 minutes by Shrewsbury and Jackson helped them make a total of 334 in their first innings. Australia lost early wickets also when they batted and had 5 wickets down for 75, however Graham scored 107 the Australians finally reaching 269.

When England batted again on the second day they had reached 113 for 2 at the close of play. On the next day England went for quick runs and they acquire 121 runs before the lunch break. Stoddart then made the first declaration of a test innings (previously this was not permitted). Unfortunately during the interval rain fell and the match was eventually abandoned as a draw. In this match Shrewsbury became the first player to reach 1,000 runs in test for England

and Grahams 100 on his debut was the first for an Australian at Lords.

On the 1st August the Australians played against a combined Oxford and Cambridge Universities Past and Present XI and made the then World Record score of 843. Trumble and Bruce were particularly savage hitting no less than 232 runs in the first 160 minutes. Trumble, Bruce and Bannerman all made centuries. The tourists however batted for so long that they denied themselves sufficient time to win the match. The Combined University side making 192 and 82 for 1 to hold on for a draw.

In this match a young Indian called Ranjitsinjhi scored 44 for the Universities. Ranjis great potential was noted but there was no question of him being selected for the test side because it was "a question of the fellows colour". However three years later the Lancashire committee asked the Australian captain at the time Harry Trott if he would object to Ranjis playing against them in the England XI. Trott confirmed the Australians would be delighted if he played as was W G Grace.

For the second test, W W Read returned replacing Flowers and Briggs replaced Peel. The match was unusual in the fact that it was the only time a test had been awarded for a Benefit Match, this was to be for G M Read who did not play in the match. England had a strong team and after Stoddart (83) and Grace (68) put on 151 for the first wicket England were always in control. England's first innings total reached 488, F S Jackson making his maiden test century (103) before being run out.

Jackson's 100 was the first in a test in England to be completed with a hit over the boundary (then worth only 4 runs).

The Australian innings lasted one hour 45 minutes and

totalled only 91 runs. Briggs taking 5 for 34 and Lockwood 4 for 37. Their second innings was much more solid affair and they reached 294 for 4 wickets, however they collapsed and were all out for 349, Briggs taking 5 for 114 and Lockwood 4 for 96. England winning the match by an innings and 43 runs to go one up with one to play in the series.

The Australians had to win the third test at Old Trafford to level the series and retain the Ashes. England's team was weakened by the injury to Lockwood and by the fact that both Jackson and Peel were unavailable, Jackson preferring to play for Yorkshire instead of England and the Yorkshire committee refusing to release Peel although they had already taken the championship title from Surrey at that time.

Australia batted first and made 204, thanks mainly to an attractive knock of 68 by Bruce. Briggs was said to have bowled "intelligently" and his 42 overs were almost half of the overs bowled in the innings that lasted for 86.4 overs, his figures were 42, 18, 81, 4. England batted and made 243 runs Gunn carrying his bat for 102 not out. In the Australian second innings they started well racing to 56 in the first 35 minutes clearing the arrears and finishing the day on 93 for 3. Bannerman was badly missed at slip by Read but when he was eighth out shortly after lunch Australia were only 143 runs in front, they did however recover slowly to total 236 all out. England had 135 minutes left to get the 196 runs needed for victory; Grace and Stoddart declined the offer and decided to play for a draw which would be sufficient to win the series and although three wickets fell late on after England had passed the 100 mark, they finished at 4 for 118 and the match was drawn.

The Australian touring party set sail on the way home on 20th September on the SS Germanic stopping off at the

United States of America on the way. The team won high praise for their conduct in the USA but there were many press stories about their conduct whilst in England and if true the disagreeable behaviour that had been reported perhaps affected the overall result.

August was to be an eventful month for Johnny Briggs, when he was playing in the match between Worcestershire and Lancashire early in the month he received a telegram and "the expression on his face when he read the contents aroused great curiosity amongst those who had witnessed him peruse the wire". It informed him that he had become the father of twin boys. Of course the news spread around the ground like wild fire and on returning to the pavilion at lunch he was greeted with the remark. "how are the twins Johnny" by several spectators.

John Briggs and his Twins.

In an amazing coincidence before the two day match had been completed Edwards the Worcestershire wicket keeper had received a similar telegram stating that he too had become a father of twin boys. A toy subsequently appeared on the market which the enterprising inventor christened "Briggs Twins". It sold well but Johnny did not receive any Royalties from the sale of the toy. In fact Johnny's brother James was "awfully annoyed at the toy appearing on the market" and stated that "if he saw anymore street vendors selling it he would cause him to show fight". Johnny could never have been accused of not taking anything in reason in good part and he was "greatly amused at James of that ilk not treating the matter lightly".

At the end of August the traditional Bank Holiday Roses match took place and it turned out to be one of the tightest finishes of any Roses battle. In brief terms 25,000 people watched the match at Old Trafford, between the top two teams in the Championship. Lancashire batted first their innings lasted for only 135 minutes in which time they scored a mere 64 runs Albert Ward batting for two hours to make 19 of that total. When Yorkshire batted they feared even worse, making only 58 runs.

Lancashire had to start their second innings at the end of the first day and at close of play it stood at 7 without loss. At the beginning of the second day Lancashire's innings lasted another 90 minutes by which time they had been bowled out for 50 runs, Yorkshire therefore requiring just 57 runs to win. The Yorkshire second innings got off to a flyer with their opening pair (Sellers and Jackson) scoring 24 runs in the first 15 minutes. Briggs was recorded as saying to Sellers "I think it's all over bar shouting". However Briggs came on to bowl and completely turned the match around. Briggs' figures for that day were 15, 8, 19, 8. Briggs took 8 for 19 and bowled

Yorkshire out for 51, and Lancashire had won by 5 runs. But it was not so much the result but the manner of the victory that was dramatic. The Manchester Guardian reported the finish of the match magnificently when it printed: "there was every indication that Lancashire was to be beaten, some great Yorkshire players were yet to bat and the runs wanted were few. There was a tremendous crowd composed almost of as a many Yorkshiremen as of the men from Lancashire. The Lancashire part of the gathering was in a state almost of despair, defeat seemed to be the destiny of the County. Crossfield at the finishing stage did a desperate thing for his side, he put on Briggs at this finishing stage to bowl, a slow bowler against punishing batsmen, but Briggs rose to the heights of this intense situation, one batsmen after another had to leave, the last partnership of all came and Yorkshire were still six runs behind. Two good strokes and Yorkshire might win the game a single bad or faulty hit and it might be lost to them, there was a breathless silence, six runs wanted, the condition was tense indeed. Then came the over of Briggs, the last over, as it happened of the day. Briggs placed the field as he willed he waved Albert Ward to a far boundary behind him right on the rails, he sent down a ball or two to George Ulyett who had stood steadily in for a long time, and on whom the hopes of Yorkshire rested. There was no score. Then he sent down the most tempting ball that a man had ever had, it appeared dearly to the natural man in George Ulyett, a very strong natural man. Every instinct in him told him to go for a huge 'swipe'. Ulyett went out to the ball sent it spinning high into the air, miles away as it seems, but it came down from the skies within the measure of the boundary. Albert Ward (resting on the rails) waited for it, the spectators gasped, Ulyett and David Hunter stood in the middle of the wicket to see how affairs would develop, the catch was made, and Yorkshire were beaten. During the long interval the people of Lancashire were sighing then they madly 'went for' Briggs and Albert Ward. It was one of the most wonderful and most delightful episodes in the history of the game of cricket."

After the match Ulyett said "I thought we were sure to win the match, I thought to myself I must try to force the fight somehow. If David Hunter had not been the last man I should have waited but I thought it better to make the runs if I could whilst I was facing Johnny Briggs, so I went for victory, but Albert Ward was on the edge of it and we lost. I still think I adopted the right course, I thought it was 100 to 1 on us winning the game at one time".

The following year when Johnny Briggs was asked what his best performance was he said "I think the 8 wickets for 19 last year against Yorkshire when we won by 5 runs. At the end of the match George Ulyett came in last. Now I thought to myself, George is an old stager, he will try to put the drag on a slow ball and get it round for 4. A great many people thought I bowled him a very slow ball indeed, but as a matter of fact it was three or four yards faster than I had bowled in the match. George had a go at it and hit it hard and straight into Albert Wards hands. I would sooner see Ulyett bat, when he is in form than any man in England".

After the match Briggs had a few drinks with some of his admirers at "the Oak" and stated that "it was not his good bowling that had humiliated Yorkshire but the state of the wicket," in fact he continued that "it was such a good bowler's wicket that he should very much like to carry it about with him".

But Cardis noted about Briggs and the match "we all of us know now that Briggs must have found many a day that it was hard to be funny. He was really a man of uncommon sensibility, his nerves were easily jarred. When he tossed his audacious ball to George Ulyett in the match at Old Trafford and Ulyett hit it deep to the long field where Albert Ward waited and caught it, the crowd mingled with his tumult of acclamation some rich chuckles of yet another 'little dodge of Johnny's'. Yet in the pavilion after the match poor Briggs sat with a white face bowling his 'little dodge' had well nigh burst his heart with apprehension". His reaction to apprehension and excitement would have consequences in later years especially at Headingly 6 years later.

Despite the remarkable feats of Briggs and Mold it was a slightly disappointing season for Lancashire even though they finished second in the table. In fact, in the summer of 1893 the Lancashire committee recognising the teams weakness had advertised for a bowler for the 1894 season adding the words "Young ones and Lancashire born preferred, a good wicketkeeper also wanted" at the end of the advert. The need for new blood at Lancashire became more important when Alex Watson decided to retire at the end of the 1893 season at the age of 48 years. The last of Briggs guiding trinity was soon to leave the scene.

In 1894 five more Counties were granted first class status, but they would not be included in the Championship until the following year, the five counties being Warwickshire, Derbyshire, Leicestershire, Hampshire, and Essex. Lancashire increase their fixtures in that year to 23 by playing Oxford University home and away plus a match at Lords against the MCC.

The retirement of Briggs colleagues and confidant put a tremendous strain on both him and Mold with regards to the bowling strength of Lancashire. Mold was to take 187 wickets for Lancashire that season and Briggs 137, the third highest wicket taker for the Lancashire was Baker with 13.

Lancashire's start to the 1894 season was once again very poor with 6 defeats and one victory in the first seven matches that they played during May and June. However Lancashire did manage to defeat Somerset at Old Trafford in a single day that year. Somerset's first innings lasted only 50 minutes by which time they had made 31 runs all out. Mold taking 7 for 10, and Briggs 3 for 16, both bowling unchanged throughout the innings. Lancashire scored 231 (Sugg 105) and then continued to bowl Somerset out again for 132 winning by an innings and 68 runs. In Somerset's innings of 132 Palairet scored 69 in a somewhat lob sided innings five other batters registering duck eggs (the terminology in those days for nought).

Lancashire played Kent again at Tonbridge that year and it was the fourth time that the town had held its annual cricket week and it was festooned with bunting. Over £200 had been subscribed by the townsfolk and there was elaborate programme of events including amateur theatricals, a smoking concert, a ball and a Venetian fete on the river. During the evening Briggs, Mold, Oakley, along with Charlie Smith went out for relaxation enjoying a row on the river Coldwell, after they had been rowing for some time, Smith happened to boast about his gymnastic ability, Briggs asked Charlie Smith to give them an example of his expertise in the sport with the aid of the bow of a tree which was over hanging the river. Smith needed little encouragement and set about using the branch as a gymnastic bar. Whilst he was in the middle of his act Briggs and Co. slowly rode the boat away from underneath the performer, leaving Smith "on his own". It is reported that Smith had plenty to say to his fellow team mates from his suspended position "but this did not subsequently prevent him from gradually relinquishing his grasp of the bow and fall in with a big splash into the river" much to the amusement of all onlookers including the oarsman.

Johnny Briggs although still only 32 years old had been playing for Lancashire for 15 seasons and in appreciation of the tremendous service he had given to the county, the committee granted him a benefit. It was to be the Roses fixtures held at Old Trafford on the August Bank Holiday weekend. The Lancashire authorities took what was then the almost unheard of step of covering the wicket with tarpaulins and made sure that it was specially cared for in order that it would be in perfect condition for Johnny's Benefit match. Briggs was arguably the most popular cricketer in the Country and record crowds were expected for the match along with record receipts to add to Johnny Briggs Benefit fund.

The Lancashire committee did everything humanly possible to honour Johnny but could not control the Manchester weather or indeed the Yorkshire captain, Lord Hawkes. Although it rained in the days preceding the match, it was fine and dry when the game was due to start, the pitch looking good and ready to last the full three days hopefully, making Briggs' Benefit a financial bumper success.

Hornby informed Lord Hawkes that the pitch had been covered prior to the game and asked him if he was agreeable to play on such a pitch, Lord Hawkes replied "certainly we will play if you allow us to bat first", adding that "he had never heard of a great match like this being played on a wicket that had been specially prepared". It was pointed out to him that on the dry prepared wicket the game would probably go to the third day but on a wet wicket it was possible that it would not. Lord Hawkes replied "I am very sorry for Briggs but I have come here to play County cricket and not a Benefit match". The large Bank Holiday crowd protested about the delay and the attitude of Lord Hawkes but he would not change his mind and a new wicket had to be cut and prepared before the match could commence. The new wicket had not been covered for the days before the match and therefore was wet and heavy.

Hornby won the toss but made what was in hindsight the wrong decision, Hornby, McClaren, Ward and Sugg had all visited the wicket and returned to the pavilion before Lancashire had registered their first run, by the time the scoreboard posted 17 runs it also indicated that 7 wickets had fallen. Lancashire rallied slightly with the help of Baker and Kemble but still only managed 50 runs in their first innings.

Yorkshire did not fare much better on their first visit to the crease at one time their score was standing at 26 for 7. Lord Hawkes was bowled by Briggs for a duck much to the delight of most of the crowd, they also rallied and it was somewhat of a stronger rally than in the Lancashire innings and totalled 152 thanks largely to the dour defence of the wicket keeper Hunter, at the end of the day it was said that Briggs had "gone home in a very bad temper". Lancashire were all out for 93 the following morning, Yorkshire winning by an innings and 9 runs. The match being concluded before lunch on the second day.

In the end Briggs received £1000 which was far from creating the expected record which would have been possible had the game lasted the full three days. Lord Hawkes tried to explain to Briggs, but all Briggs would say was "I do not wish to speak to you My Lord". Briggs also required a great deal of persuading not to return Lord Hawkes donation of one guinea. However it was reported afterwards that "it must not be forgotten that Lord Hawke was especially kind and thoughtful to Briggs afterwards and the little chap was always the last in the world to bear malice against anybody".

The wicket which had been carefully prepared for Briggs' Benefit, came into use later in the week when Kent was the visitors. This game lasted three days Kent scoring 225 for 7 in the second innings to win the match.

In the Sussex match at Old Trafford that year, there was a somewhat surprise appearance of the 51 year old Alfred Shaw, seven years after his last match for Nottinghamshire, he had qualified for Sussex by residency and took 4 for 52 in the match. Shaw was to retire back to his native County to Gedling, Nottinghamshire. His life-long cricketing colleague and business partner Shrewsbury also retired to the same village. Shaw died in 1907 but Shrewsbury believing that his worsening asthma and failing sight would prevent him playing cricket again, shot himself in 1903 within a year of his last first class appearance. Shaw and Shrewsbury are buried within 30 yards of each other in Gedling.

Some other notable figures by Briggs his Benefit season were as follows

With the bat
65 v Surrey
51 v Surrey
59 v Oxford University
101 v Kent
61 Players v Gentlemen

With the ball
7 for 44 v Oxford University
7 for 46 v Surrey
6 for 47 v Surrey

7 for 91 v Yorkshire
6 for 27 v Leicestershire

There were three winter tours at the end of 1894, Lord Hawkes leading a short tour of 5 matches to North America with one of those matches being played in Toronto. The reason the tour was of such a short duration was that the two Oxford men Mordaunt and Bardwell had to be back in time for the start of the new term.

The second tour was to the West Indies and was led by R C Lucas. This was the first tour to the West Indies and the all amateur side was by no means up to first class county standards. The trip was mainly a social one and the cricket was not taken too seriously. The same cannot be said of the third tour that winter the one to Australia.

It was to be the first time the authorities in Melbourne and Sydney would join together to promote an English team in Australia. A E Stoddart captained the team, the full team consisting of the following players -

A C Maclaren	Lancashire
F G J Ford	Middlesex
H Philipson	Middlesex
L H Gay	Somerset
And the professionals	
T Richardson	Surrey
W Brockwell	Surrey
W H Lockwood	Surrey
A Ward	Lancashire
J Briggs	Lancashire
R Peel	Yorkshire
J T Brown	Yorkshire
W A Humphreys	Sussex

This side did not include W G Grace, F S Jackson, R Abel or W Gunn, so the batting was not at full strength. W Attwell did not go either but apart from his absence, the bowling was the first choice. The team left for their 24 match tour from Tilbury aboard the Ophir on the 21st September 1894. It was on this voyage MacLaren was to meet and fall in love with his future wife, the Australian Socialite Maud Power. On arrival in Australia the Society Columnists were to comment on the "Scottish named member of the team who was Miss Powers devoted companion throughout the voyage". The team stopped off to play a match at Colombo, Ceylon on their way to Australia. They played a Colombian XIII and beat them by 18 runs, Johnny Briggs taking 6 for 6 in Colombian's first innings.

The first match after arriving in Australia was against an XVIII of Gawler on the 3rd November. England had the best of the draw having scored 368 in their first innings whilst Gawler's reply totalling 153 (Briggs 10 for 94) they then stood at 22 for 5 in the second innings when the game ended.

In between this match and the first test at Sydney a shooting party had been organised for the tourists. Briggs, Ward, Richardson, Lockwood, Brockwell and Brown were the team members who elected to go on the nights sojourn. Certain members of the team refused to go out with the party of guns when they knew Johnny Briggs was included in it. The touring members were accompanied by C Hennessey, F W Groom, J Tolmie and E J Dann and started out from Hennessey's Queens Hotel initially to enjoy Mr Handley's hospitality at Paradise Farm, Near Drayton and from there to go on for "a little opossum shooting". They all carried guns apart from Richardson who volunteered to carry the spoils, they also had in their possession a large amount of ammunition. Mr Handley was the guide and he soon found them a possum. There was a stampede to see who could kill the first possum.

When they finally caught sight of the possum, they all fired in the general direction of the creature, Brockwell with his sixth shot fell the possum, and claimed the first kill.

Some of the English team had never seen a possum before and they were keen to see what it looked like and what they were shooting at. Next they encountered a bear and Brown, Lockwood and Ward all emptied both barrels. The bear had to fall.

They had a very eventful night and returned with a large bag. On one occasion Ward stated later that he was "looking forward and found Johnny's gun pointing dangerously at his head, he was walking in front of me with the barrel over his shoulder. I called his attention to this but he confidently assured me it was quite alright as the trigger was only half cock".

Whilst the party were gathered around discussion the shoot, there was a large bang that came from the direction of Johnny's gun, the resultant shot whizzed past the gathered members, rather too close for some, and they enquired "what did you shoot at Johnny?" Johnny said a "native cat", nothing could be seen, but there was a lot of long grass about near the edge of the fence, so Johnny was given the benefit of the doubt. The party returned to Paradise Farm where Mr and Mrs Handley had prepared supper for them. After this they left for Toowoomba after giving three hearty cheers for Mr and Mrs Handley. On arriving back at the Queens Hotel, they were greeted with loud applause as they entered the hotel with their spoils. They were then entertained to a Smoke Concert by the townsfolk, and at 12.00 midnight the evening was brought to a close, everyone joining together to sing "Auld Lang Syne".

The first test match took place at Sydney starting on 14th December and it was to last for six days. It was the tourists' ninth match of the tour and it turned out to be a magnificent and thrilling match. England fielded four debutants J T Brown, F G J Ford, L H Gay and A C MacLaren, Australia five, J Darling, F A R Iredale , E Jones, C E Mcleod and J C Reedman. Australia won the toss and batted first. Richardson had a sensational start for England seeing Lyons, Trott and Darling all returning to the pavilion dismissed off his bowling the score then standing at 21 for 3. Giffin and Iredale, with the help of drop catches by Gay, the wicket keeper, stood firm, the fourth wicket not falling until the score reached 192. Australia ended the day in a strong position of 346 for 5. On the second day, more dropped catches demoralised the England bowlers and Australia amassed 586 runs. Gregory becoming the first player to score a double century (201) in Australia. When England batted they lost three wickets for 78 but managed to reach 130 without further loss on the second day. It rained over the weekend which did not help the wicket. Nearly all the England bowlers contributed to the score and when Blackham the Australian captain and wicket keeper, had to retire with a split finger, the Australia fielding became a little ragged.

Ward (75), Briggs (57). Brockwell (49) and Gay (33) helped England to a total of 325. England however had still to follow on being 261 runs behind Australia.

England fared better in the second innings and with a solid 117 from Ward, cleared the arrears still having 6 wickets in hand. Again a good all round performance by the later batsmen. Brown (53), Brockwell (37), Ford (48) and Briggs

(42) pushed England's total up to 437 ensuring that the Australians had to bat again. The total set for victory for the Australians was 177. The pitch was still in good order and by the end of the day the Australians had reached 113 for 2 in their victory chase. To all intense and purposes the match was lost to England, Australia only needing 64 runs the following day with 8 wickets in hand. Peel was one of those who had given the game up and he decided to have "a few beers" during the evening. "A few beers" was to be Peels undoing later in life and would lead to his expulsion from first class cricket in 1897 when Lord Hawke, his Yorkshire captain dismissed him from the field after seeing him bowling at the side screen and urinating on the outfield, he did not play another first class match after that incident. It rained heavily during the night and by time the teams arrived the next morning, the sun was beating down. Peel and Co. were not really in great shape that morning, but after a cold shower and with the agreement of the Australian captain, the start was delayed so that Peel could sober up and take part in the game. When Peel had arrived late at the ground, he was reported as saying "Give me t'ball Mr Stoddart and ah'll get t boogers out before loonch".

The third Australian wicket fell at 130, Darling caught by Brockwell off Peel. By this time the uncovered wicket, which had been saturated overnight was almost unplayable. Briggs trapped Griffin 135 for 4. 42 was still needed. Briggs and Peel then tightened the screw. Iredale was caught and bowled by Briggs, Gregory was caught behind by Peel and Readman stumped after charging down the wicket to Peel. 18 to win 3 wickets left Turner was caught at cover point by Briggs off Peel, and Jones in the deep by MacLaren off Briggs bowling. One wicket left with 15 needed. Blackham who had made 74 runs in the first innings before splitting his finger, placed himself down the order in the hope that he would not be needed to bat Macleod then nudged a single here and there, trying to protect the injured Blackham, but in the end Blackham provided a catch back to Peel, and England had won by 10 runs minutes before lunch on the sixth day. At that time it was the only instance in test cricket of a team winning after being forced to follow on.

For the second test the teams travelled to Melbourne, for a game that would span the New Year period, starting on 29th December 1894 and finishing on the 3rd January 1895. For Australia Blackham was still injured so Griffin took over the captaincy and Jarvis the wicket keeping duties. Coningham was also brought in to the team. After Gay's dismal performance behind the stumps at Sydney, he was replaced by Philipson, in the England team, which then remained unchanged for the whole of the series.

Heavy rain before the match had soaked the wicket, Australia won the toss and asked England to bat, on a wicket that would no doubt help the bowlers, particularly on the first day. When England batted MacLaren was caught by Trott off Coningham, the Australian debutant, off his very first ball in test match cricket. He was to take 2 for 17, in the first innings, did not take a wicket in the second, and in fact he did not take another test wicket or play in another test after this. As far as England were concerned from then on, it was a sorry procession, with Ward making 30 and Stoddart 10, out of England's total of 75 runs compiled in two hours. The heavy roller was then applied and although the wicket improved slightly Australia soon found themselves in trouble at 15 for 3, but recovered to make 123 in their first knock. The wicket was then rolled again by mutual agreement for a further 15 minutes, and it was hoped that the wicket might improve over the Sunday break.

England cleared the arrears in the first hour on the Monday morning with the loss of MacLaren's wicket. Ward, Brown and particular1y Stoddart played well and England had reached 239 with 6 wickets by stumps on the third day. Although Stoddart played magnificently to score which was then the highest score for England in a test 173, the second innings was predominantly a team affair. One member scoring over 20, four members over 30 and one over 40. I suppose that one could argue that they got out just when they were getting in, but all their contributions gave England a second innings score of 475. Australia needed 428 runs to win and made drastic changes to the batting order in order in the hope of achieving this total.

G H S Trott was moved up the order to open the batting with Bruce, the move seemed to have worked well when Australia reached 191 before the fall of the second wicket, but they then fell away reaching 268 for 9, Iredale and Turner then added 60 runs to that total before the end of the fourth days play, but could only manage 5 more runs the following morning when Iredale was bowled by Peel. Australia had made 333 but England had won by 94 runs and went two up in the series.

The third test at Adelaide was played on the 11th, 12th, 14th, and 15th January in Intense and overpowering heat, which the tourists in particular had difficulty coping with, it was to be a vital game which Australia had to win to stay in the hunt for the rubber. The England team was unchanged, but the Australians gave debuts to J Harry and A E Trott, the brother of G H S Trott. England were totally outplayed by Australia, and with the intense heat and frequent rain showers, the England fielders tired rapidly even in the Australians first innings. If it was not for two run outs, and the magnificent bowling of Richardson, Australia would have made far more than their total of 238. England moved Briggs up the order to open, but this gamble never really paid off. They collapsed to 64 for 6, finally making 124, the Australian lead was then 114. There had been an amendment to the follow on rule, which increased the margin to 120, otherwise England would have batted again when the wicket would have been at its best.

At the end of the second day Australia had made 145 for 4,259 runs on. With the English fielders weakening under the heat a 140 from Iredale and a 72 not out from A E Trott, the Australians posted a total of 411. This total was to be far out of reach of the visiting team and England were bowled out for 143 in their second innings, the Australians winning by a massive margin of 382 runs.

MacLaren noted in later years that "when a thunderstorm stopped play in the third test at Adelaide, who was it, for the hours we had to spend in our dressing room, entertained us with a fine rendering of Macbeth, but Johnny Briggs. How we laughed, but he went on as if it was going to rain until doomsday, never pausing for a word or to take breath. We told him he had missed his vocation and had thrown away a Cesarewitch. He still went on. For a long time it puzzled me why Johnny should have committed to memory so much Shakespeare and wondered if he had contemplated chancing his arm on the stage when it had lost his cunning in the cricket field".

In the Adelaide match the Australian debutant A E Trott, scored 110 runs, without being dismissed and had bowled in the heat throughout the second innings, taking 8 for 43. A E Trott, played in the remaining two tests of the series, and it was with astonishment that in the following year he was omitted from the team to tour England which was to be captained, by his brother, G H S Trott. He emigrated to England qualifying for Middlesex, he played for them for many years and had a Benefit Match in 1907. In this match played against Somerset, he took four wickets in four balls, and then three in three balls, a double "hat" trick, in the same inning. He stood as an umpire early in the 1913 season, but his health deteriorated and he had to retire from the game, aged 42 years. He could not bear life without the game he loved so much, and on the 30th July 1913, he shot himself.

The teams moved back to Sydney for the fourth test, due to start on 1st February.

Stoddart won the toss, and put the Australians in to bat on a wicket that had suffered badly from the recent rain. In fact this was the second wicket that had been prepared for the match, bad weather completely ruining the first one. Peel and Richardson bowled well, and when Australia stood at 51 for 6 and with Peel and Briggs well in command, Stoddart looked to have made a wise decision. Darling then came in and with the fielders visually wilting, hit out. Several chances were to be put down and when Darling was next out, the score stood at 119 for 7 and the game had changed. Graham and A E Trott then added 112 before Graham was out, Trott finishing on 85 not out. The last four Australian wickets added 233 runs to make Australia's total 284. Johnny Briggs figures in the first innings were 4 for 65, he had Graham and Gregory stumped by Philipson, took a return catch from Iredale and had Jarvis caught behind for his fourth and final wicket. With the fall of this wicket Johnny Briggs became the first bowler ever to take 100 test wickets. England had to face only a few minutes in the field that day by which time MacLaren had been stumped by Jarvis. It rained all day on the Saturday, so no play was possible. There was no play scheduled for the Sunday, and although the day was bright it again rained heavy on the Sunday evening. England once again moved Briggs up the order to first wicket down with MacLaren and Ward opening, the Lancashire colleagues occupying the first three places in the batting order. Unfortunately Stoddart's prediction that "we shall be out twice in one day" proved to be correct. England scored 65 and 72 and the Australians won the match by an innings and 147 runs squaring the series.

C T B Turner playing in his last test match became the second bowler to take 100 test wickets after Briggs, and he was therefore the first Australian to complete the task.

For the final test at Melbourne, the public interest could not have been higher and with a perfect pitch throughout the match no team was to gain an advantage by batting first or second. It was to be a very even match, the result in doubt until right up until the final stages.

England were unchanged again, but the Australians brought in Lyons and McKibbin for Moses and Turner. Turner who had taken his 100 test wicket during the previous test was one of the three selectors for this game and it was said he was over ruled by the other two, Blackham and Griffin, and was omitted from the team.

Australia won the toss and elected to bat making a solid start at 124 for 2. However they were reduced to 152 for 4 just before tea, but then thanks to some sterling batting from Gregory and Darting recovered to post a score of 282 for 4 by stumps on the first day. Both went early on the second day and it was 286 for 6. Lyons hit a quick 55 and the tail wagged somewhat. Australia making 414 in their first innings. When England batted they lost Brockwell at 6, but Stoddart and Ward put on 104.

Similar to the Australian knock, it was the middle order that was to prove to be the backbone of the innings. MacLaren who had an injured finger scored 120 in a stand of 162 with Peel. England stood at 328 when the fifth wicket fell but unfortunately the tail went limp. England were all out for 385, a deficit of 29 runs. Australia made 69 for 1, by the close of play on the second day. Australia started well on the third morning, their score standing at 124 for 2 at one time. Peel and Richardson changed ends, the Australians were then made to fight for every run. Their sixth wicket fell at 200 and they progressed to make a final total of 267 leaving England to score 297 to win the match and the series. Brockwell again went cheap, late on at the end of the fourth day and when Stoddart was dismissed with the first ball of the next day, England were 28 for 2. However Brown and Wards third wicket partnership of 210 set a new test record for any wicket at that time. Brown (140) scored his first 50 in 28 minutes. It is doubtful whether many 50s have turned a game so completely or many stands so vital in achieving a test match and series win. England in the end won comfortably by 6 wickets. The rubber was won but only just and the feeling was that with his excellent batting line up, two first class spinners and a pair of great fast bowlers in Lockwood and Richardson, Stoddart's task should have been easier.

However on the tour Lockwood had only took five test wickets at 68 each whilst Richardson claimed 32 for an average of 26, the problem lay in Stoddart's inability to bring the convivial hard drinking Lockwood to heel. Unfortunately in those days, whether good, bad or indifferent, a player was virtually certain of his place as there were only thirteen members in the party and the reserves, which in this case were a wicket keeper and a lob bowler, not a very satisfactory situation.

It was the lob bowler Humphreys that was bowling in a up-country match of little consequence when Brown and Briggs who were the wags on the tour asked if they could field for a few overs near the leg side boundary, this they did and when a catch was offered to that part of the ground, they were nowhere to be seen, they were in fact in the refreshment tent drinking lemonade. Humphreys stated that he definitely needed men in that position. When another catch went to the same area of the ground Humphreys was surprised that such an easy chance had been dropped by Briggs, always noted for his excellent catching ability. It was only after a close inspection that he realised that Briggs and Brown had again gone back into the refreshment tent for more lemonade, lending their caps to two spectators who were only too pleased to help the two absentees and field for England. The 42 year old Humphreys was not amused.

The interest shown back in England in the test match series was greater than for any previous tour, and it finally established the domination of the "test" in the programme of English teams visiting Australia. The tourists played four more matches after the last test, before setting sail for England, and arriving back at Plymouth on the 8th May 1895.

On the domestic front the five teams that were granted first class status the year before, Warwickshire, Derbyshire, Leicestershire, Hampshire and Essex all played in the Championship for the first time in the 1895 series. The Championship then consisted of 14 teams.

Lancashire appointed MacLaren as captain, for that season, but he had been on the winter tour to Australia and decided to come back via Japan, consequently missing the first two matches of the season. He did however play in the matches against Leicestershire and Yorkshire, but when the opportunity came for regular employment and what's more regular income, he took himself off to be a Preparatory School Master at Harrow.

Lancashire had three different captains over his seven match absence before MacLaren had returned for the game against Somerset at Taunton starting on the 15th July. MacLaren had been at Lords the day before watching the Eton and Harrow game and had travelled down to meet up with his father who was to be present at the Somerset game. MacLaren won the toss and elected to bat, he opened the Lancashire innings, with his fellow test player and tourist Albert Ward and at lunch the Lancashire score stood at 141 without loss. Ward went soon after lunch when MacLaren was joined by Paul; together they put on 363 runs in 190 minutes, before Paul was caught in the outfield when he had scored 177. The close of play score was 555 for 3 with MacLaren's contribution standing at 289 not out. On the second day MacLaren continued in the same majestic mood he was 404 not out at lunch and Lancashire were 756 for 6. He went on to make 424 batting in total for 7 hours and 50 minutes, hitting one 6 (it had to be out of the ground in those days), 62 - 4s, 11 - 3s, 37 - 2s and 63 singles, and his four centuries came in 155, 105, 90 and 94 minutes. Lancashire's final all out score was 801.

Briggs took 4 for 59 in the first Somerset innings and 5 for 78 in the second.

Lancashire winning by an innings and 452 runs. The Somerset captain of the day, S M J Woods, the Australian test all-rounder, was later to write in the Cricketer Magazine, "we started what I may call a busy week in July (1895), that is from a bowlers and fielders point of view. Essex scored 692 in their only innings, three of their batsmen got 100s and another

99. We lost by an innings and 317 runs. We rested on the Sunday and lost the toss on Monday against Lancashire. A C MacLaren kindly consented to play against us. He went in first and scored 424 in a marvellous manner, we were beaten by an innings and 452 runs. A nice weeks cricket don't you think"! MacLaren was only 23 years old when he performed this feat at Taunton.

Lancashire had three or four players that were to figure for the first time in 1895.

Lancaster. Hallam and J T Tyldersley, the most important addition was to be John Thomas who was to develop into both the most popular and the prolific batsman of his day and was to exceed 1000 runs in a season 19 times. His 2,633 runs in 1901 remains a Lancashire record. Lancashire came second in the Championship that year behind Surrey. Their success was mainly due to the batting of MacLaren and Ward and the bowling of Mold and Briggs. Mold took 182 wickets for his county, Briggs 119. Among Briggs bowling feats that season were the following

8 for 49 v Gloucestershire
8 for 17 v Leicestershire
7 for 67 v Nottinghamshire
6 for 48 v Surrey
and 5 for 62 v Yorkshire

7: The Declining Years
(1896 to 1898)

A NEW SYSTEM for deciding the Championship was to be introduced for the 1897 season in which draws were ignored and losses deducted from wins, the final position being determined by the percentage of points gained in finished matches.

For Lancashire MacLaren was again not available until July. Therefore Hornby who was now in his 50th year again captained the team in the opening match which was to be against Yorkshire at Old Trafford on the 4th May. One newspaper reported that "it was a pleasure once again to see the veteran Hornby on the field with unimpaired activity and the same insatiable desire when batting to run out his partner". The match against Yorkshire very nearly didn't take place, there was a dispute between the counties about the date of the first match because Lancashire, not unreasonably, wanted to give the Whitsuntide fixture to the visiting Australian tourists. This was a departure from tradition which Yorkshire resented. Lancashire then accused Yorkshire of discourtesy in their correspondence. So heated was the exchange that Lancashire made the correspondence available to the Manchester Guardian and the Sporting Chronicle and until the breach was healed Kent were prevailed upon to visit Old Trafford each August Bank Holiday, this arrangement continued for several years until better relations were established across the Pennines.

When the match did take place it started in cold and windy conditions. Anybody who has watched a match at

Old Trafford at the beginning of May will know what that really means. Lancashire batted first and struggled, only Sugg making many runs, scoring a masterful 74 out of his team's total of 150. Paul on 16 was the next highest scorer. When Yorkshire batted they were, not for the first time it has to be said, battered by Briggs who took 5 for 44 in their first innings which totalled 123 runs. Lancashire went in a second time making 139, thanks mainly to a 52 from Paul, this setting Yorkshire a total of 167 for victory.

Their attempt to hit off the runs was a heart stopping affair, Mold took early wickets but first Brown and then Denton stayed with Jackson. When the latter two were together victory looked certain for Yorkshire, but when Jackson went, quickly followed by Moorhouse the victory was less certain. Mold then bowled Wainwright and with Mounsey and Hirst at the wicket Yorkshire were struggling, the clock crept slowly round with neither attack nor defence giving way, the pair still there at close of play, Yorkshire having two wickets in hand and still needing 18 more runs for Victory. The weather was much better the following morning, with the sun shining and less wind Mounsey and Hurst managed to knock off the required runs without alarm, giving Yorkshire Victory by two wickets.

When Gloucester played at Old Trafford that year W G Grace carried his bat, scoring an unbeaten 102 runs. When Lancashire batted MacLaren had made two when he either trod on his wicket or knocked the bails off when setting off for a run, the umpire refused the appeal on the grounds that the Lancashire captain had completed his stroke and had started to run, the good doctor was not amused stating that "MacLaren was out and he knew he was out" and he went on to demonstrate to the umpire what had taken place, several minutes were taken up in discussion about the incident, Grace being reluctant to accept the umpires decision as final. An extra 10 minutes was taken for lunch, no doubt in heated argument about the event. Grace was jeered by a selection of the crowd when leaving the field for arguing with the umpire. Near the end of the match and close of play Lancashire needed 30 runs to win in their second knock which started at 6.15 pm. Grace however was still in a disgruntled mood and wanting to get a quick departure at the end of the match, fielded in his everyday clothes, it was reported that "he looked even bulkier than ever as he stood at point in his ordinary attire".

Contrary to "tradition" Lancashire had a good start to the season and victories over Sussex, Kent, Leicestershire, Derbyshire, Warwickshire, Surrey, Somerset and Gloucester had placed them second in the table to Yorkshire, by the end of June. However they could not improve on that position during the season, eventually finishing second again in the Championship.

Willis Cuttell joined Lancashire that season but did little in his first match, the Yorkshire game at Old Trafford. He was however to figure more fully in coming years. Lancashire won eleven of their 22 matches that year, MacLaren averaging 54 in the half of the season he played and Sugg 39, while Briggs (145 wickets) and Mold (137 wickets) again carried the bowling, although Hallam made a useful contribution with 58.

Briggs contributions that season also included

Bowling
6 for 38 v Somerset
6 for 44 v Surrey
5 for 14 v Warwickshire
5 for 44 v Yorkshire

4 for 36 v Australia (for Lancashire)
6 for 41 v Australia (for North of England)
Batting
54 v MCC
60 v Kent
74 v Kent

It had been the fifth time in 7 seasons that Lancashire had been runners up in the Championship, but with Briggs and Mold along with Sugg and Ward, Lancashire were beginning to assemble a strong and balanced side and it was almost inevitable that the first prize would be gained sooner rather than later. The Australians visited England in the summer of 1896 and although they were to play a total of 34 matches on the tour in England they also played at Colombo on the way out and after leaving England played several matches in America before crossing the Pacific and playing another 5 matches in New Zealand before finally returning home, to Australia.

They left Adelaide aboard the SS Cuzzo setting sail for England on 14th March 1896 and arriving during the third week of April. The first test match was to be their thirteenth match of the tour and was to be played at Lords on 22nd, 23rd and 24th June. England had given a debut to A F A Lilley, Briggs did not play in this match. Australia gave debuts to C J Eady, C Hill and J J Kelly.

The first mornings play was probably one of the most sensational in test cricket, with over 30,000 people crammed into the ground. The Australians won the toss and decided to bat. Donnan ran himself out when the score was 3 and Griffin was caught behind by Lilley off Lohmann without addition to that score. One run later Richardson knocked out Trott's middle stump, his pace being irresistible and when he took Gregory and Graham's wicket in successive deliveries Australia were reduced to 26 for 5. Eventually the Australians were bowled out on a fast, dry wicket for 53 runs in 75 minutes. Lohmann taking 3 for 13 but Richardson doing the main damage with 6 for 39 all six cleaned bowled.

In the England first innings Stoddart went for 17 when the scores stood at 38, the second wicket fell at 143 and even though the fifth wicket did not fall until England's score stood at 256, they fell away somewhat being all out for 292. This still gave them a commanding first innings lead of 239. The Australians second innings started just after midday on the second day. Donnan was injured so the opening pairing were Darling and Eady. Darling was bowled without a run on the board and when Eady was caught behind with the score on three a repeat of their first innings looked possible, they did however manage to reach 62 before Griffin fell to Richardson. When Gregory joined Trott, who had recorded a Duck Egg the day before, they transformed the innings, scoring 90 runs before the lunch break and 131 after, in a record fourth wicket partnership of 221. Trott finally making 143 and Gregory 104, unfortunately for the Australians this momentum could not be continued by the later batsmen and Australia's final total of 347 meant that England had to bat again and to score 109 to win the match. 16 of these were made late on for the loss of Abel's wicket. Rain fell overnight and what seemed a straightforward job for England became more difficult. They did however reach the total with a loss of only three more wickets but the Australian fielding was somewhat at fault and if the chances had been taken England may well have struggled even more. England scored 111 for 4 in their second innings, winning by six wickets and going one nil up in the three match series. In this match Jones first ball to W G Grace was a short pitched delivery which lifted sharply and passed through the great man's beard, deceiving the keeper and going straight on to the boundary.

For the second test at Old Trafford the Lancashire committee selected MacLaren and Ranjitsinhji to replace Hayward and Gunn and brought in Briggs for the injured Lohmann.

A STUDY IN LEGS.

By "RIP."

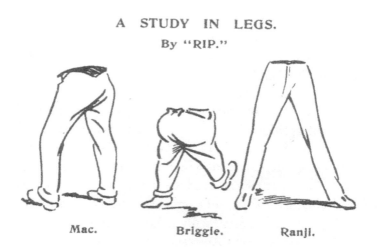

Mac.   Briggie.   Ranji.

This meant that England were relying on only three front line bowlers. Australia again won the toss and on a perfect wicket and against a limited attack, chose to bat, they scored 366 for 8 on the first days play. Iredale and Griffen putting on 131 for the second wicket. When Iredale was out with the score at 242, Trott and Gregory looked as if they were going to repeat their Lords effort. In desperation Grace decided to give Lilley, England's wicket keeper a bowl. In order to do this Brown was switched to take over wicket keeping duties. Lilley's bowling was awful, going for 23 runs in five overs. He did however achieve his captain's objective and broke the partnership having Trott caught behind the wicket by Brown. The next morning the ninth wicket added 41 and Australia's final total was to be 412. When England batted a good 62 from Ranji and a top score of 65 not out from Lilley helped keep the deficit down to 181, England making 231 in their first knock. Following on England, lost Grace, Stoddart, Able and Jackson before stumps that day, the fourth wicket falling at 111. When England lost their sixth wicket on the last day, they were still two runs behind the Australian first innings score. Ranji who by this time had reached 50 in 85 minutes then raced to his 100 in 2 hours 10 minutes and with help from the tail-enders remained unbeaten on 154 when the England innings closed on 305. Australia started their second innings at 2.50 pm needing only 125 to secure victory.

There was no tea break in those days so Richardson bowled without rest and at one time when the Australians stood at 100 for 7, the result was in the balance, however Richardson's 6 for 76 was not enough and the task was to prove too great, Australia reaching their required total with 3 wickets to spare.

Ranji in this match was the first Indian to play test cricket, becoming only the second batsmen after W G Grace to score 100 on his debut for England. He was also the first player to score 100 before lunch in a test match when on the third morning of the match he took his overnight score of 41 not out to 154 not out, adding 113 runs in 130 minutes.

There had been some unrest in the England camp concerning match fees and when the Surrey committee announced the team for the next test, five of those selected wrote to the committee stating that they wanted a match fee of £20 instead of the £10 they had been paid at Lords and Manchester. The committee refused even to negotiate with them. Of the five complainants Abel, Hayward and Richardson withdrew their demands, but Gunn and Lohmann refused to, the latter two being left out of the team.

After Briggs disappointing figures of 2 for 99, and 1 for 24 at Manchester, he was not selected for this match, Richardson and Hayward being partnered by Peel and Hearne.

The first two tests had been remarkable ones and it was sad that the third and final test at the Oval was to be adversely affected by the weather. There had been rain prior to the day of the match and heavy showers on the match day delayed the start until approximately 5.00 pm on the first day. England won the toss and decided to bat; on a slow wet wicket in poor light, England did well to reach 69 for one by stumps on the first day. The wicket had "turned nasty" on the second day and with the score at 114, the fourth wicket fell. Trumble changed to the Pavilion End and the last six wickets fell for 31 runs in 50 minutes. England totalling 145 in their first innings.

When the Australians batted, Darling and Iredale put on 75 runs in the 45 minutes either side of lunch, when Iredale, going for a fifth run was magnificently run out by Ranji from a distance of over 100 yards. The rot set in and the last nine Australian wickets fell for 44 runs, Australia making 119. England batted for the second time and in the last 85 minutes of the day, struggled to 60 for 5. 22 wickets fell on the second day whilst 210 runs were scored. The match was then in the balance and with a lead of only 86 much would depend on the weather and the state of the pitch the following day. If anything the pitch deteriorated overnight and the batsmen on both sides had difficulty coping with it. Three England wickets fell at 67, one at 68 and England were all out for 84 in their second innings, a lead of 110. When Australia batted a second time, amazingly they lost their first nine wickets for only 25 runs, but a 16 by McKibbin helped them reach 44, they did however lose the match by 66 runs and the rubber two to one.

During this series many people were not happy with the bowling action of both Jones and McKibbin and "deplored the relaxed standards", that allowed them to go unchallenged throughout the season.

The Championship of 1897 right up to the end of July looked as if it might make the Authorities at Lords the object of ridicule. Nottinghamshire at that time had played eleven matches and won only two of them, but topped the Championship table, because the remainder of their matches had been drawn. As draws were excluded from the reckoning it means that Nottinghamshire had 100% record. Luckily the eventual winners were not to be crowned until the end of August that year and so spared the Authorities blushes. For Lancashire MacLaren expressed a wish that he would like to be removed from the Captaincy and the 50 year old Hornby again took over. It is said that bowlers win titles and Lancashire badly needed support for Briggs and Mold, who had carried the side through the 1890s. Both had taken more than 100 wickets each in the years 1891 to 1896. But support was badly needed for them if Lancashire had any chance of clinching the Championship. Support did come, firstly in the unlikely form of the 32 year old Willis Cuttell who took over 100 wickets that season and Albert Hallam who took over 90. Briggs was way out in front with 140, Mold took 88, this despite being troubled by injury. Lancashire were to have four bowlers finishing the top 12 of the national averages that season.

On the 10th and 11th June Lancashire entertained the visiting Philadelphians at Old Trafford, the Lancashire spectators were given a rare chance to see the American J B King, who was one of the greatest fast bowlers in history, in action. The Philadelphians made 123 in the first innings (Briggs taking 5 for 77) and 86 in their second. Lancashire 149 and 64 for three, winning by seven wickets.

Lancashire had made an ideal start to the season, they beat Derbyshire, Hampshire, Leicestershire, Middlesex, Derbyshire again and drew with Nottinghamshire.

Lancashire played Essex for the first time in ten years and the game at Leyton contained some unpleasantness. Lancashire were in trouble in a wearing wicket and Mold was at the crease, there was every possibility that they would have to follow on, meaning that Essex would have had to bat last, by which time the wicket could have been very difficult indeed. Fred Bull the Essex off-break bowler made every effort to give runs away, so that Lancashire would not have to follow on and consequently Essex would not have to bat last on a turning wicket. Bull bowled deliberately wide giving a number of runs away, Mold was not to be fooled by Bull's actions and after a number of wide balls, he decided that Bull was not going to get away with those types of tactics, so he deliberately hit his own wicket to make sure that Lancashire had to follow on. Heated discussions followed during the interval and at one time Hornby refused to continue with the game, however Bull admitted that he had bowled wide on purpose, apologised and the game continued, Hornby said after "I have been connected with first class cricket over 30 years and have never seen such as disgraceful thing in connection with the game. Indeed, I was completely amazed when I saw Mold had knocked his wickets down, and could hardly believe it, but when I heard the explanation and Bull admitted what he had done and apologised to me, I could not blame my men. But it is not my idea of playing cricket.

Under the circumstances, which I hope will not occur again whilst I am playing cricket, I think Mold was justified in his action, although personally I should never agree to anything of that sort being done".

Essex had made 290 in their first innings, Lancashire 168 when Mold was out, "hit wicket". Lancashire did follow on and made 251 in their second innings, leaving Essex 130 for victory, both Bull and Mold were to be proved wrong concerning the deteriorating wicket. Essex winning comfortably by six wickets. The first of the Roses matches that season was played at the Park Avenue ground, Bradford, and it was the Yorkshire wicket keeper David Hunter's benefit match.

Yorkshire batted first scoring 345, Lancashire replied with 354 which included a superb innings of 152 from MacLaren. It looked for all the world that the game was going to peter out into a dull draw on the third day. Cuttell (4 for 44) and Hallam (4 for 17) had other ideas and Yorkshire were quickly reduced to 36 for 7 and then 51 for 8. Haigh and Hunter then dropped anchor and although Yorkshire were bowled out for 66 in their second innings, time had run out for Lancashire and the match finished in a draw.

In the second match at Old Trafford on 12th, 13th and 14th August, Yorkshire won the toss and decided to bat. Jackson making a handsome 59 out of a Yorkshire total of 160. Lancashire batted and reached 213 for 7 when Cuttell joined Sugg he went on to make 44, Sugg finishing with 122 and Lancashire 286 a lead of 126. Briggs and Cuttell then got amongst the wickets in the Yorkshire second innings with 4 for 46 and 5 for 31, respectively. Yorkshire were bowled out for 100, Lancashire winning by an innings and 26 runs. More importantly the win for Lancashire had moved them to top of the Championship, Surrey were then second and when the two teams met on the 19th August at the Oval it seemed whoever won this match would more than likely lift the Championship. There were 30,000 people on the opening day of the match and it was the Surrey and England fast bowler Richardson who caused Lancashire problems all though the match. Bowling in poor light he laid out MacLaren, broke Wards and Sugg's bat and broke Sugg's finger, Briggs was hit three times, Lees Radcliffe was lamed, Ward also suffered and Tyldesley faced one over from Richardson in which every ball whizzed past his head. Lancashire had won the toss and decided to bat; they reached 140 for 4 at lunch, with Sugg 50 not out. After lunch the fifth wicket fell at 147, Lees and Richardson then quickly finished Lancashire off, bowling them out for 154, the last 6 wickets falling for 8 runs.

Surrey made 216 a lead of 62, Lancashire had made 68 when the second wicket fell but when Sugg retired with a broken finger, when he had scored 37, the innings fell away and Lancashire were bowled out a second time for 151. Surrey required 90 runs for victory and completed their task with the loss of four wickets.

Lancashire had lost by six wickets and when they drew the match at Lords their title chance looked to have gone and that they might have to settle for second place in the Championship once more. However, Lancashire winning eight of their last eleven games and losing only to Essex and Surrey and drawing at Middlesex put themselves back in the shout of the Championship. Lancashire could still win the Championship if they could win their last match against Nottinghamshire, but Surrey only had to avoid defeat against Somerset to clinch the title. The matches between Lancashire and Nottinghamshire and Somerset and Surrey both commenced on the 26th August.

In the Lancashire verses Nottinghamshire match at Old Trafford, Lancashire won the toss and decided to bat, in a solid performance, several batsmen reached double figures and Lancashire reached 284 in their first innings. Nottinghamshire totalled 120 in their first innings, Briggs taking 4 for 66 and Cuttell 5 for 45, when they followed on Briggs bowled a single over whilst Cuttell with 7 for 36 and Hallam 3 for 84 bowled throughout the Nottinghamshire innings in which they made 124. Lancashire obtaining victory by an innings and 40 runs. All eyes then turned to Taunton and the Somerset and Surrey match.

Somerset had won the toss and batted, having a disastrous start their innings at one time standing at 21 for 6, however a solid innings by Robson of 48, saw them reach 110. The Surrey innings mirrored the Somerset one somewhat, when they stood at 19 for 6, their Saviour was Lees with 41, but they still fell short of the Somerset first innings by 17 runs making 93. Somerset second innings was a more workmanlike performance, 8 players reaching double figures in their total of 193, this leaving Surrey to get 210 for victory. Although they started well, the second wicket not falling until the score was 62, the sixth wicket had fallen by the time the score had reached 73. Lee and Wood made a brief fight back but Surrey were all out for 144. Somerset had won the game by 66 runs and had given the title to Lancashire who were outright winners for the first time since 1881. That year they had a balanced attack rather than relying on two main bowlers. In the overall first class averages all four of the main bowlers came in the top 12, taking 420 wickets between them in the season, their record in purely Championship games reads

	M	0	M	R	W	Ave
J Briggs	26	1149	340	2294	140	16.54
W R Cuttell	25	1039.2	418	1813	102	17.70
A W Mold	20	759.2	261	1571	88	17.75
A W Hallam	26	952.4	421	1651	90	18.31

Johnny Briggs average of 16.54 runs per wicket included the match at Old Trafford against Sussex where he not only bowled the most balls in a match, 630 balls, but also conceded the most runs in a Championship match, 306. He bowled 126, five ball overs taking 2 for 174 and 2 for 132 in a match which somewhat spoiled his seasons average. This was partly due to his captain, MacLaren who was at times "stubborn to the point of near stupidity and would never acknowledge his faults". When Briggs was taking punishment in this match he insisted in persevering with him and when the crowd eventually shouted to MacLaren to change the bowling, he threw the ball angrily and pointedly to Briggs, at the end of each over, for him to continue, as if to emphasis his position as captain. Not that this action was to concern Briggs for he was to say to his captain after being hit a few times and wiping his global forehead with his handkerchief. "It's a fine day Mr MacLaren", and continued to bowl. Briggs had bowled better than he had for some years and he was rewarded with a place in Stoddart's side that would tour Australia in the coming winter.

The party set sail for their 22 match tour from Tilbury on 17th September, 1897, except for Ranji who joined the side later. Although the team stopped at Port Said and Colombo, no cricket was played at either, and they arrived at their destination on 25th October 1897. The full party that accompanied Stoddart was -

A C MacLaren	-	Lancashire
J R Mason	-	Kent
N F Druce	-	Surrey
K S Ranjitsinhji	-	Sussex

Professionals

T Richardson	-	Surrey
T W Hayward	-	Surrey
J T Hearne	-	Middlesex
J Briggs	-	Lancashire
J H Broad	-	Gloucestershire
W Storer	-	Derbyshire
E Wainwright	-	Yorkshire
G H Hirst	-	Yorkshire

On the outward sea journey the team suffered an influenza epidemic and many of the team were far from well when they arrived in Australia. In their first match against South Australia in Adelaide, Clem Hill played a brilliant innings of 200 for the home team to which Ranji replied with 189, the match was conveniently declared a draw after only a couple of hours play on the fourth day, this enabled the team to fit in a visit to the races which was to include one of the most famous horse races in the world the Melbourne cup.

The first test match was due to start on 10th December in Sydney, but the Authorities postponed the start until the 13th December because of the rain that had fallen on the previous days. The decision to postpone the match was taken without consulting either captains and Stoddart made a formal protest about this, though in fact the postponement helped England's cause, since Ranji was still unwell with the after effects of influenza and a throat infection. Stoddart then received news of his mother's death in England. Stoddart who was devoted to his mother was very badly affected by this death and the rest of the tour became a sad chore, to be completed as soon as possible, certainly there was no chance of him playing in the first test, despite the postponement. MacLaren was therefore to captain England for the first time.

Ranji had recovered from his throat infection and was included in the team. England scored 337 for 5 by the end of the first day. MacLaren reached his 100 just before tea when Ranji was 39 not out but virtually exhausted. He received medical treatment overnight and was well enough to continue the next day, he made 175 before being last out when England's score stood at 551. Australia then made 86 for 5 by the end of the second day and lost an early wicket the following morning at 87 for 6. Australia recovered some ground thanks to a 70 from Trumble and 50 not out from McLeod, who batted with an injured hand that he had received fielding, they totalled 237,314 runs behind England. When Australia batted a second time, they changed the batting order, Darling opening with Iredale. Darling was 80 not out at stumps. McLeod came in first man down and his dismissal caused ill feeling between the two opposing teams. He was bowled by a no ball and as McLeod was deaf he never heard the no ball call from the umpire, McLeod walked, Storer the wicket keeper replaced the bails only to remove them again with the ball and run McLeod out; apologies tended afterwards were eventually reluctantly accepted. Australia's second knock totalled 408, this leaving England to make 95 runs for victory. This they achieved with the loss of Mason's wicket, winning by nine wickets and going one up in the series. During the match, it was noticeable that the Australian skipper did not bowl Jones from the end at which Jim Phillips was umpiring. Phillips who was travelling with the England team as umpire, had no-balled Jones for throwing in the very first match of the tour and was a self-appointed scourge of doubtful action. In those days, it was only the bowler's umpire who could call a no ball. Briggs figures in the match were 1 for 42, in the first innings and 2 for 86 in the second, 3 for 128 in the match.

From Sydney the team moved North to play against a XVIII of Newcastle, here the mosquitoes bit everyone, it was stated that "Hirst presented the appearance of a prickly pear", one of Mason's eyes was completely closed and Stoddart's face and hands were quite "globular". It was no wonder Stoddart looked so bad for it was later discovered that the uncured skin of a large sea bird had been placed under his bed for drying purposes and this was found to be harbouring various kinds of small insects.

The second test at Melbourne started on New Year's day, Ranji had made an agreement with the Australian authorities to absence himself from the first days play only in order to visit a doctor to have his throat abscess lanced. The match was played in exceptionally hot weather, even for Melbourne, and winning the toss was to prove vital. Australia won the toss and decided to bat, they batted for the greater part of two days, McLeod, making 112 and after Australia had made 283 for 3 at stumps on the first day, they went on to total 520 near the end of the second day. England then batted for approx 30 minutes making 22 for one at the close. During the long Australian innings MacLaren was criticised for not bowling Wainwright, who had done the double for Yorkshire the previous season, when the regular bowlers were exhausted in the heat. There was a sensation the following morning when Jones was no-balled by Phillips. It was the first time a bowler had been no-balled for throwing in a test match at Melbourne. It was an isolated call and Jones action was normally regarded as fair.

In the England first innings Ranji batted with ease and when the score stood at 202 for 4, they looked to be in with a chance in the match, but Ranji was out just after tea and it needed a late stand between Briggs (46 not out) and Druce (44) to take England past the 300 mark and register 315, by this time the wicket had deteriorated and had cracked up so badly that Noble (6 for 49) and Trumble (4 for 53) had no trouble in bowling England out a second time for 150. The Australians winning the match by an innings and 55 runs, levelling the series.

During this tour the England team was subject to ghosted press articles, one of which concerned Johnny Briggs, he was to comment later that "no greater calamity was ever uttered than when the Australian press sought to prove that dissension existed amongst us. It was a downright falsehood. Our misfortune on many occasions appeared to more strongly cement the bonds of good fellowship". He went on to state that "a representative of the Melbourne Argus newspaper, called upon me to express my opinion on one of the test matches, I declined to see him, but under pressure came down and told him he had seen the match and if he had any qualifications as a critic his own judgement would pull him through. Judge my surprise next morning, when in large type, there appeared 'Briggs interviewed', and a column of matter appeared. This from a man to whom I had only said a few words, indignant, I went to the Manager asked for some explanation, told him it was not only badly written but unauthorised. I had to accept the usual remedy a profuse apology. This is a sample of what has often been levelled at us, in Australia".

The teams then moved on to Adelaide for the third test, due to start on 14th January 1898.

England made one change, Stoddart taking over the

captaincy again with Wainwright stepping down. For Australia, Howell a medium pace off-cutter, replaced McKibbin.

Australia won the toss and decided to bat, Australia reached 310 for 2 at the end of the first day in 285 minutes. Darling was to pass his century mark with a huge hit off Briggs, this going out of the ground for 6. The first 6 every recorded in a test match at Adelaide, he was to carry on to make 178 before he was finally caught behind the wicket off Richardson. The Australians batted on into the third day and amassed 533 runs. When England batted, the wicket was perfect but they slumped to 42 for 4, recovered to 197 for 6 and with a 70 from Hayward and an 85 from Hirst managed to reach 278 all out. Following on 295 runs behind England lost Mason on 2, but MacLaren and Ranji put on 142 for the second wicket, MacLaren going on to make 124 and Ranji 77. Unfortunately for England the next highest score was to be a 27 from Druce in England's second innings total of 283. Australia winning by an innings and 13 runs going two one up in the series.

Besides the problems with ghosted press articles on the tour there was also some unsavoury barracking from the crowd on the tour. Johnny Briggs was to comment on barracking in general and in particular the Adelaide match, "on every ground in England principally at Lords, the Oval, Old Trafford and the Yorkshire Grounds, I have met crowds in many different moods, sometimes despondent, other times enthusiastic. But the sense of fair play is one we all admire, and in difficulties, or otherwise we feel sympathy. Not so in Australia. 'Barracking' would never be tolerated in England. In 1886, when I visited Australia for the first time barracking was in its infancy, indeed cricket was less progressive than now and crowds were not such mammoth proportions. Possibly the most disgraceful exhibition of barracking was witnessed at Adelaide. The principal suffer was Prince Ranjitsinji, who felt acutely the repeated insults and reference to his colour. It matters little to me what goes on as long as the game is being played properly".

The fourth test was to be played at Melbourne commencing on 29th January and with the rubber at stake England brought back Wainwright for Hirst, who had been injured. The Australians fielded an unchanged team, again won the toss and again decided to bat.

The wicket had been covered for the game and England got off to a superb start thanks to the opening bowling partnership of Hearne and Richardson, the latter bowling faster than he had done all the tour. Australia were soon in trouble, being reduced to 32 for 5, when Hill just recovered his ground and avoided a run out. Trott was out soon after lunch when the Australians score stood at 58 for 6, the Australian innings was in ruins and Hearne's figures at that time were 4 for 20. The absence of the injured Hirst started to tell on England after lunch with both opening bowlers having to continue long after they had tired. It was then that Hill aided by Trumble and then Kelly played the innings of his life, he reached his 100 in 2 hours 49 minutes and scored 182 not out on the first day, adding only six runs the following day, this was the highest score on the first day of a test in Australia and his partnership of 165 with Trumble was the best seventh wicket stand against England. The first six wickets had fallen by the time the score had reached 58, the seventh fell at 223. Australia totalling 323 all out. In stifling heat England batted feebly and were all out for 174, seven batsmen getting into double figures but no large innings by any of the England players. England fared better in their second knock and at one time a close finish looked a possibility, but it was not to be, England being bowled out for 263, setting Australia 115 to win. This they achieved with the loss of two wickets, winning by 8 wickets and securing the rubber.

Fierce bush fires around Melbourne had filled the air with smoke when England batted a second time and some blamed this for England's second innings failure. So dense was the smoke when they followed on that the ball could not be seen from the press box. Briggs remembers the match and mentioned it in connection with umpiring. Johnny stated "In the fourth test at Melbourne when we were batting the light was so bad that we considered it was unfair to play. However after finishing our first innings, I happened to be 21 not out and as we had to go in again our captain asked Wainwright and myself, to open the second innings. It was close on time, perhaps half an hour to play and on-going out Mr Stoddart asked me to appeal against such a wretched light owing to a bush fire, first speaking to Trott, good fellow as he is, he seemed to sympathise but was powerless to intervene and we then had to appeal to the Australian umpire, Charles Bannerman, who had a short consultation with 'our umpire' Phillips, who was supposed to voice our interest but the order came back to play on, and, angrily enough we had to submit to the inevitable, a glaring piece of business, uniformly condemned". The reporter who interviewed Briggs was to speak to him again at a later date when he stated that "the liable laws prevent me from using all he (Briggs) told me respecting the umpires".

In between the fourth and fifth test matches the England team played a New South Wales side at Sydney in early February. The match scores and result was as follows:- New South Wales 415 and 574, England 387 and 363. New South

Wales winning by 239 runs. The 1739 runs scored in this match was a record aggregate score for a first class match.

The fifth and final test was to be played back in Sydney starting on the 26th February and concluding on 2nd March. For this match Hirst returned for England with Stoddart standing down, MacLaren was to captain England in his absence. Worrall replaced the out of form Iredale for the Australians. This time England won the toss and decided to bat. The decision looked a good one for it was not until England reached 111 did they lose their first wicket that of MacLaren. Unfortunately Wainwright and Ranji soon followed at 117 and 119, but Storer the wicket keeper and Heyward put on 78 and then a fine knock by Druce (64) meant England closed the first day on 301 for 5. However the next day Jones came out of the traps quickly bowling splendidly to take 4 wickets for 11 runs. The last five England wickets falling for 34 runs.

When the Australians batted for the first time, Richardson took a leaf out of Jones book and bowled brilliantly, he was at last free from the rheumatism that had plagued him all tour and he took 8 for 94 in the Australian innings which totalled 239. England having a first innings lead of 96.

In the second England innings MacLaren was out first ball, Ranji was out LBW to a ball he believed he had touched first and the first ball Storer received he claimed was a definite throw. England were then 30 for 3 and went on to make 178 leaving the Australians 275 for victory.

Darling the Australian opener decided attack was the best form of defence and went after Richardson, just before his 50 came up Richardson changed to bowling round the wicket at him, he thought he had him LBW, but Richardson had run in front of Bannerman the umpire, un-sighting him and he was bound to say not out. The incident caused unrest in the crowd which had been an unpleasant feature on the tour on more than one occasion. Darling continued to play well and hit the fastest 100 ever recorded against England reaching three figures in only 91 minutes. His knock contained 20 4s, his great innings of 160 helped Australia reach their target with six wickets in hand. Darling was the first batsman to score 3 100s in the test rubber and the first to aggregate over 500 runs in one series. This was to be Richardson's last test match. The match concluded on 2nd March 1898.

On the 17th March that year, MacLaren was to marry Kathleen Maud Power, the second daughter of Robert Power, the Irish born and extremely wealthy director of the Dalgety Pastoral Empire, and one of the founders of the Victoria Racing Club. The wedding was the highlight of the social calendar and the local gossip columns made the most of it. A combination of a handsome cricket captain and a wealthy land owner's daughter was too good to miss.

Sir Arthur Priestly was the best man and the Rev, Cannon Tucker conducted the service. The church was decorated with floral wickets, bats and balls and the bridesmaids were to wear the red rose of Lancashire and carry bouquets in the Stoddart's team colours. All the touring team were in attendance at the function. Johnny Briggs was to state that "it was a very pretty and smart function" and that "it seems so unique for one of us to take this step on tour".

The Wedding Party.

It might well have been "a very pretty and smart function", but before the ceremony the "irreverent and indecent crowd" had surged into the church taking up every possible vantage point including the pulpit. During the service the Rev Tucker twice admonished the congregation for "standing on the pews and chattering". At the end of the ceremony the crowd surged all over the church, tearing down the decoration in an effort to secure a floral souvenir. In the words of one social column "the sanctity of the Holy House was for once forgotten".

Afterwards at the bride's father's residence in Toorak near Melbourne, Johnny Briggs stated that "we pledged over a glass of wine very hearty wishes for their future happiness and success". MacLaren and his new wife then went on to Governors and Lady Brassey's vice-regal residence of Healesville for a brief honeymoon before re-joining the other cricketers at Port Adelaide for the voyage home aboard the SS Ormuz. The professionals arrived back in England by the overland route through France on the 23rd April, the amateurs choosing to continue by sea, arriving a few days later all except Ranji who had left the boat at Colombo.

Concerning the tour Wisden was to observe a year later that "there has not for a long time been anything so disappointing in connection with England cricket as the tour of Mr Stoddart's team last winter. The team left England in September 1897 full of hope that the triumph of three years before would be repeated, but they came home a thoroughly beaten side". Wisden was to add that "the Colonial players were much more consistent in batting and far superior in bowling".

Stoddart was to recover from the loss of his mother but in 1915, aged 52 years, besieged by financial worries, ill health and an unhappy marriage, he shot himself.

The 1898 domestic Championship season, was to be a great disappointment for Lancashire after their Championship winning effort the previous year. This was due to a number of reasons. MacLaren played only six championship matches. Even then his form was poor, his average being less than half of the previous year at 23. Mold missed a match in July and then broke down again in August with a knee injury. Hallam did not play all summer. Hallows was crippled by a strain and Briggs who had a disappointing tour in Australia taking only 9 test wickets at the cost of 53 runs each, seemed stale and out of touch, his 79 wickets costing 24 runs each that season. The bowling problem was so bad for Lancashire that they asked the 51 year old Alex Watson to turn out for them after an absence of five years, Watson very wisely refused. It was the first time in the last 12 years that Briggs had failed to take over 100 wickets in a season. Until the middle of July, Lancashire though always behind Yorkshire, were well placed in the table and if Yorkshire had slipped up and Lancashire continued winning they may well have retained the title, but as it was they were beaten successively by Essex, Yorkshire and Sussex, and finished the season in sixth place. In the end it turned out to be a very poor season for Lancashire, winning only 9 of their 26 matches, losing 6 and drawing the remaining 11. Yorkshire won the championship.

Lancashire and Briggs could only hope that the 1899 season with the visit of the Australians would bring them greater success. This hope turned out to be ill founded, for Briggs in particular, in a dramatic fashion.

8: The Tragic Years
(1899 to 1902)

JOHNNY BRIGGS WAS a true character, a rubber ball of a man, full of life, a will of the wisp of a fellow, a comedian and clown, both on and off the field, like so many funny men there was a darker side to his personal, private and family life. Johnny Briggs mother's aunty was insane, his daughter was classified as an imbecile and his father was an alcoholic, who at this time was the landlord of the Queens Arms, Moor Lane, Widnes.

The Briggs family at Stand.

Johnny was looking forward to the New Year with excitement and anticipation, but early in 1899 his father James Briggs became ill.

He had a previous attack of pneumonia six years earlier and had never really fully recovered from this illness. After a prolonged bought of severe pneumonia, which lasted approx. 6 weeks, he died on the 18th February 1899, at his residence at the Queens Arms, Widnes, at the age of 61 years.

Although Doctor Edwards with Dr Dreachfield (Manchester) and Dr Hal Abram (Royal Infirmary, Liverpool) were the consultants and had made sure everything possible was done for him, it was to no avail, he left a widow, three sons and two daughters.

James Briggs was a leading light in the sport of cricket in the Widnes area, coming to Widnes, 22 years earlier to be the professional at the Widnes cricket club, also holding the joint post of groundsman. He held these positions for 17 years.

After ending his connections with the club, he started his own club Briggs C.C. He introduced a new feature to local cricket, that of a matting wicket.

The funeral at Farnworth church was very well attended. The service was conducted by Rev. W. Thatcher BA. The chief mourners were his family Mrs Briggs, Joe Briggs, John Briggs, James Briggs, sons, T Briggs And A. Briggs, daughters, and H. Hardy, brother-in-law. There were approximately 40 other mourners representing various other cricketing clubs, and wreaths were placed in the form of cricket bats and balls and cricket wickets and bails.

The 1899 season was again to be a disappointment to Lancashire and their supporters, finishing fourth in the Championship, with 33.33 points. It was the tenth official running of the Championship. Surrey won the championship with Middlesex second and Yorkshire just ahead of Lancashire in third position.

Worcestershire were admitted to the championship for

the first time that year, bringing the total number of counties to 15. Surrey won the title with 66.67 points. Only 5 teams had plus scores one team Essex recorded a zero score and 9 teams with a minus score tally. Derbyshire being the bottom team with minus 63.64. Yorkshire played the most games with 28, Nottinghamshire the least with 16. Points were awarded as follows. One point for a win, one point taken away for a loss, the points were then divided by the number of matches completed (i.e. those that ended in a win or a loss) and then multiplied by 100.

Lancashire's best result that year was the 59 run win at Sheffield (Bramhall Lane) in the Roses match at the end of June.

There was a great deal of excitement and a certain amount of trepidation concerning the arrival of the touring Australian team led by J. Darling.

Australia 1899. Back row: V. T. Trumper, H. Trumble, A. E. Johns, W. P. Howell, B. J. Wardill (manager), M. A. Noble, F. Laver, C. E. McLeod. Middle row: J. J. Kelly, C. Hill, J. Worrall, J. Darling (capt.), F. A. Iredale, E. Jones. Front: S. E. Gregory.

This was to be the first time England had hosted five, three day test match series. Prior to this series the English team had always been selected by the host grounds committee; for example, if the match was to be played at Old Trafford, the Lancashire committee would pick the test team; this could lead to favouritism concerning local players. This time the team was selected by a group of selectors for the first time. The three appointed selectors were, Lord Hawkes, W G Grace and H. W. Bainbridge. Grace was chosen to lead the team but the 50 year old was past his best and it was sad to see and hear some of the Trent Bridge crowd criticising Grace's poor and clumsy fielding.

The match held on 1st, 2nd and 3rd of June 1899 at Nottingham and it was to be Grace's last test match.

Briggs was not selected for this match due to his lack of form. The new selectors were unlucky when it transpired that Lockwood, Richardson and Kortright, for various reasons were all unavailable, the match was a dull affair with the Australian's taking all of the first day to score 238 for 8. Their innings ending on 252 the next morning. In England's first innings of 193, C B Fry top scored with 50, Australia scored 230 in their second innings which closed at lunch on the last day. Leaving England to score 290 to win. England settled for the draw but Ranji hit out near the end in a vain attempt to reach his century, giving an unusual display for a man trying to save a match. He ended 93 not out when the match ended in a draw.

Some old masters. (Drawing by "RIP!")

The second test match that year was played at Lords on the 15th, 16th and 17th of June. Grace's long run in the England team had come to an end and he was replaced by the Lancashire captain A.C. McLaren. England scored 206 in the first innings which was always a below par score, England were always in trouble after the Australians registered 421 in their first innings, with both Hill and Trumper scoring 135 each. A magnificent 88 in the second innings by McLaren could not rescue the England team who ended up losing the match by 10 wickets. Johnny Briggs was still overlooked for selection, in this match.

With the poor results at Lords and Trent Bridge, something had to be done to restore confidence and improve the performance of the England team. McLaren lobbied hard for the selection of Briggs who he argued was coming back to form. The next test match was to be played at Headingley in Leeds. It was to be the first test match staged at that ground. The match was scheduled for 29th, 30th June and 1st July, but both McLaren and Briggs were to play in the Roses match held at Bramhall Lane, Sheffield, the three days immediately prior to the third test.

In the Roses match McLaren's 126 in the first innings for Lancashire and Briggs 7 for 76 in the second ensured that Lancashire won by 59 runs and seemed to confirm McLaren's view that Briggs was back in form. Briggs was selected for the third test at Leeds, and he was over the moon, for he knew he was coming to the end of his long career and he had already 94 Australia test wickets under his belt. It was his ambition and hope to increase that tally to 100 during the match at Leeds. The paying crowd of 19,815 went wild with excitement when the teams entered the field. The atmosphere was electric, the Australians won the toss and decided to bat first, Briggs opened the bowling, and he became the first person to take a wicket in a test match at Headingley, Leeds when he had Kelly caught by Fry for one when the score was 8.

Wickets continued to fall during the day, Briggs claiming two more, the Australian captain Darling for 9 caught by Young when the score was 114 for 5 and had Laver stumped by Lilly for 7, becoming the eighth wicket down when the Australian's score had reached 151 for 8. The innings ended when Howell was caught by Ranjitsinji off Young, when the score was 172. Briggs figures for the innings were 30-11-53-3. When Darling was dismissed he had hit the ball hard to mid-on, and it looked for all the world that a boundary would result, however Young went up "like a clockwork figure" and the ball stuck. Briggs could hardly contain himself while Young thought it "quite a matter of everyday occurrence".

Before the end of the Australian innings Briggs was fielding when a great tragedy occurred.

The excitement had got the better of Briggs and he had a severe epileptic fit and seizure on the field of play. He was immediately taken to the Club house where a doctor was quickly summoned.

He recovered slightly in the early evening enough to join the Australian and English teams on a visit to the Empire Palace Music Hall in Leeds.

On the evening of the first day of the match the 29th June, several members of both the England and Australian teams visited the Empire Palace Music Hall in Leeds at the invitation of the Management to watch a variety show. Top of the bill were Ludwig Amman and Millie Hylton along with other supporting acts such as Fanny Dango.

Their known presence at the concert ensured that the theatre was full and a tremendous atmosphere was created by their presence at the concert. Briggs was amongst the England Cricketers attending that evening. It was thought he took his seat in the front row of the Grand circle. The evening was going well until about 10 o'clock when Briggs then had another violent fit and seizure and after a struggle was carried out of the theatre by his team mates and friends.

In fact it appeared that he had arrived late and finding no seat in the Grand circle stood at the back with Brockwell and a number Australians. It was commented on how ill he looked, his face being drawn and haggard. At the time of his fit it was noted that his eyes "stared out of his rigid face", this obviously caused a commotion among the theatre goers and quite a number of them started to assemble outside the theatre to find out what was happening to poor Johnny.

Briggs was immediately taken by cab to the home of Mr F. Bagshaw, one of the Vice Presidents of the Leeds Cricket Club, at Ash Grove, Headingley, where he was attended to by Mr J.L. Iredale, Surgeon of Woodhouse Lane, Mr Iredale later announced that Johnny was the victim of a massive Epileptic seizure caused by nervous excitement. Johnny lay unconscious for a number of hours and had a succession of seizures during the night. He was seen at various intervals during the night by a Doctor but as late as 3.00 pm on the Friday afternoon he remained unconscious. Briggs' condition continued to cause grave concern so it was decided to contact his relatives who duly arrived in Leeds from Widnes, late on Friday evening. His wife and his children were not well enough to attend. She was in a delicate state of health and the children had Scarlet Fever.

Mr Iredale suggested that the immediate cause of Briggs breakdown was the excitement and the strain of the test match. This was indicated by the gestures and motions of Briggs picking up or bowling a ball whilst still in an unconscious state. McLaren went to see Briggs late at night and was struck by the fact that Johnny knew him but did not recognise his own brother. McLaren was also concerned about using "his interest with the selection committee to get Briggs chosen for the game". He also commented that "it is not pleasant to think that however indirectly my action had a result that no one could have foreseen, the excitement proved too much for Briggs and sent him off his head".

Briggs left Leeds in a first class carriage of the London and North Wales Express at 1.20 pm on Monday 3rd July 1899 bound for his home in Manchester. When he entered the train carriage he was smoking a large cigar and looked in excellent health. He was accompanied to Manchester by both Mr Iredale and Mr Bagshaw along with a Lancashire friend, Mr French of Lytham. On arriving at Manchester he was asked by a reporter about his health, to which he replied "I am very much improved, thank you". He then proceeded to his home at 15 Stamford Street. Near the Old Trafford cricket ground in Stretford, Manchester.

The following day the 4th July, much to everyone's surprise, Briggs arrived at the Old Trafford ground to watch the Lancashire v Sussex match. In view of his condition and the instructions to him to have complete rest, it was probably not the best move to make especially when he was confronted by a large number of well-wishers congratulating him and enquiring about his health. It was noted that Briggs appeared to be anything but well and evidently not by any means recovered from his Epileptic Fit in Leeds. He left the ground with Mr French and travelled with him to Mr French's home in Lytham. It was hoped that he would find more peace and rest there. Briggs was admitted to Cheadle Royal Asylum the following Saturday 8th July 1899.

Meanwhile back at Headingley the test had continued with the children playing cricket around the ground, with the bowlers putting soap into in their mouths, to re-act the demise of poor Johnny. The match ended in a somewhat disappointing result when England stood in a strong position. The test continued after Briggs' tragic departure on the first day and was not without incident. Australia scored 172 in the first innings, England's reply was 220.

Australia's second innings began quietly reaching 34 without loss, then Young had Worrall caught by Tyldesley (sub for Briggs) in the outfield. Hearne came on and bowled Hill for 0, then had Gregory caught by McLaren the very next ball and Noble caught by Ranji to complete his hat trick, the Australian's were reduced to 34 for 4. This was the first hat trick in a Test match in England. Godfrey and Noble both registered "a pair of spectacles" two duck eggs in the same match. The Australian's then lost another wicket and at 39 for 5 were in some trouble, still 9 runs behind England's total. Trumble (56) and Laver (45) then came together with a stand of 73 enabling the Australian's to post a total of 224. England required 177 runs to secure victory, they went into bat late on the second day and scored 19 without loss at the close, this left them to score 158 runs, with all wickets intact, (minus Briggs) on the third and last day. Rain fell on the last day, and not a ball was bowled. The match was therefore drawn.

Briggs was discharged from the Lunatic Asylum after approx. 8 months on 28th March 1900 in time for the start of the 1900 season. It was to be the final season that Briggs would play for Lancashire.

The touring West Indies played at Old Trafford in 1900 and although the team were made up of Amateurs, the Manchester City newspaper commented "that with a little more experience they will have to be taken into serious account before long". Briggs took 7 for 43 in that match, this season he was to bowl over a thousand overs, taking 120 wickets at 17.4 a piece.

Other notable match figures of that year were

8 for 51 against Derbyshire,
5 for 22 against Kent,
5 for 35 against Middlesex and
7 for 53 against Nottinghamshire

His finest achievement of the season however, would be against Worcestershire, this was the first season Worcestershire had entered the championship and therefore the first time at Old Trafford.

A large crowd was not expected for the visit of Worcestershire but as the opening day fell on Thursday 24th May which coincided with the public holiday for the birthday of Queen Victoria a crowd of 7,000 attended the first days play. H.K. Foster the Worcestershire captain did not gain much by winning the toss and deciding to bat, his side were reduced to 70 for 7 at lunch. All the 7 wickets falling to Briggs, Briggs stated at lunch that it was "his intention to commemorate the Queen's birthday by bagging the whole lot". Two more wickets fell immediately after lunch, both to Briggs. Bird 33 and Straw 7 not out then batted with care from 3.00 pm to 3.30 pm putting on 32 runs before a Bird ran out to on drive, Briggs missed the ball and was bowled. Worcestershire were all out in their first innings for 106. Briggs returned figures of 28.5 – 7 – 55 – 10, it was noted that "His old command over the ball seemed to have increased rather than diminished over the years".

When Briggs returned to the pavilion he was met with "great cheering from the crowd". It was only the seventh time all 10 wickets had been taken in an innings and only the second time by a Lancashire player. Worcestershire made a better fist of it in the second innings with H.K.Foster scoring 113 in a total of 253. Lancashire had scored 205 in their first innings and needed 155 to complete the victory. Lancashire lost the first five wickets for 82, however Tyldesley, 71 not out and Eccles 39 not out, saw the host club home by 5 wickets. Lancashire were to finish second that year, behind Yorkshire in the championship.

On Christmas Day 1900, Johnny took part in a benefit/charity football match at Old Trafford between Old West Manchester and Herbert Turners team, Briggs was asked to kick off the match.

Being an ex-rugby player Briggs gave the ball an almighty kick and the crowd shouted "no ball". It was probably one of the most funny matches on record, Briggs commented that the contribution of Will Farrell, the Irish comedian made him "feel like laughing for a fortnight".

Early in 1901, Johnny Briggs went to his place of business which was Pilling and Briggs Sportswear in Oxford Street, Manchester, and ordered Mrs Pilling's son Douglas to take all the bats out of the rack, place them on the floor and oil them. This operation was not needed or necessary. He then ordered the printers to send the sports catalogues back, which had been ordered by Mrs Pilling; these had just come in and were needed for the shop. Briggs then had a severe fit in the shop and needed restraining.

Briggs was re-admitted to Cheadle Royal Asylum on 8th March 1901, he was said to be in an "excitable, semi-unconscious condition". The next day he was in seclusion for 12 hours with maniacal excitement and after that for 10 hours a day. He used to hold conversations with imaginary people and claim that his food was being tampered with.

On 22nd March he had been sectioned for 10 hours and his speech was rather thick. Over the following few weeks he had delusions of grandeur and claimed he was the best jockey in England.

On the 9th April he stated that his wife and the Queen were in a bag and he was keeping people from them. He improved slightly and was taken to the front gallery in the Asylum on 28th April. If you behave well you were taken to the front gallery, on a bad day you would be removed back to the Second back gallery, out of sight and sound. After a few days in the front gallery he was indeed returned to the second gallery on the 9th May. Whilst in the Asylum Johnny used to bowl at imaginary batsmen, mainly those from Australia and Yorkshire, noting the scores and his bowling figures at the end of each day

When in the Asylum he also took part in inter club cricket matches arranged by Cheadle Royal, several times he scored a century and played against a strong team brought in by Hornby, the old Lancashire captain. The spectators thought he was as well as ever, but those who knew Johnny well knew differently, he was a shadow of his former self.

On the 6th June 1901 Briggs wrote to Mr Sam Swire, at Old Trafford the following letter:

Dear Sir

I am finally willing and fit to play for the Red Rose on Monday 8th June and am in good form. I shall be able to give the other bowlers a bit of a rest and it makes me feel quite unhappy at the result of the last match.

Yours obediently

John Briggs

PS. You might see Dr Philip Mould and tell him that I am feeling fit and well.

During September of that year he was having hallucinations. On the 1st of November he had a convulsion attack and it was noted he had started to wet the bed. He was then in daily seclusion for 10 hours a day. On the 8th January 1902 it was noted that "he looked very dull and heavy during the last few days and convulsive". On the 10th January his fits continued and he fell into a deep coma, it was noted at that time his pulse was very weak.

The next day 11th January 1902, at 12.00 midday, Briggs quietly passed away. One of the greatest cricketers of the day, if not ever, breathed his last. His cause of death was certified as Cerebral Disease for about two and a half years (general paralysis of the insane) by W. Scowcroft, W.R.C.S.

9: Epilogue

BRIGGS' FUNERAL WAS to take place on Wednesday 15th January 1902 at 2.00 pm in Stretford Cemetery, Manchester.

It was one of the largest funerals that Manchester had ever seen. A.N. Hornby invited a number of prominent cricketers to meet at the Queens Hotel, Manchester at 12.00 midday before the funeral, they would then go to Oxford Road Station where a special train would take them to Stretford.

The party left for Stretford about 1.30 pm, included in the party were

Rev. J R Napier, O P Lancashire, H R Rowley, S H Swire, A Appleby, E Roper, R G Barlow, A Watson, W Gunn, L Hall, G Yates, G Nash, A G Paul, W Sugg, H Bagshaw (Leeds) Dr P Mould (Cheadle Royal).

The open-top hearse brought the body directly from Cheadle Asylum and was due to depart from Briggs' house at 15 Stamford Street at about 1.00 pm. A crowd of well-wishers and sympathisers began to gather at the house about an hour before the departure time, by the time the cortège was due it was recorded that there were about 1,000 people present in the street. As soon as the cortège arrived at his house, the chief mourners started to enter the carriages.

In the first carriage was Masters Jack and George Briggs (sons), Messrs. Joseph and James Briggs (Brothers), Mr John and C.H.Burgess (brothers-in-law). There was no record of Johnny's wife, Alice attending the funeral.

The second carriage contained Mr J Hardy (uncle), Messrs. J.T and H. Burgess and Master T Harrison (Nephews), Master Douglas Pilling and Mr A. Timperlay.

gates about 2.00 pm. The service was conducted by Rev. J.R. Napier who was a former member of the Lancashire County cricket team.

The cortège drew up at the mortuary chapel, the coffin was taken from the hearse to the Chapel by Alderman Quinn and Councillors Laws, Smith, and Palin followed by the mourners. After the service, the coffin was taken from the chapel to the graveside by six of the late cricketer's professional colleagues, A. Mold, G. Yates, F. Sugg, A. Paul, G. Smith and A. Ward. The route between the chapel and the graveside was lined with people, 6 or 7 rows deep, the scene was noted as "impressive in the extreme". It was also commented on that "such a widespread magnification of sorrow at the death of a public man, is very rare, and the ceremony will not lightly soon be forgotten by those who took part in it".

I leave the last appropriate moving words to Mr G.A. Hodcroft who wrote in his book "My Own Red Rose", about Johnny Briggs, when he stated:

"In an age when people's ideas of Heaven are undergoing radical changes, and when even Christian Bishops are telling us that we must not believe literally the conception of a perfect existence beyond the vale of tears, I still like to think that in some Elysian Field, where it is always high summer and where one day we may watch the immortals of cricket in action again, Johnny Briggs, bubbling with infectious laughter and zest for the game, will be taking his two little steps to the wicket and diddling out the best of them, as in his great and happy years".

THE END

BIBLIOGRAPHY

- *A history of Australian Cricket* – Chris. Harte
- *A history of County Cricket - Lancashire* – John Kay
- *Archie - A Biography of A.C. Maclaren* – Michael Down
- *A Sportsman's Memories* – Edward Roper
- *Bat and Ball - A New Book of Cricket* – Edited by Thomas Moult
- *Cricket Facts and Feats* – Bill Frindall
- *Cricket in Firelight* – Richard Binns
- *Cricket's Silver Lining* – David Rayvern Allen
- *Cricket's Strangest Matches* – Andrew Ward
- *Days in the sun* – Neville Cardus
- *England Test Cricketers (a complete records from 1877)* – Bill Frindall
- *From The Stretford End - The Official History of Lancashire Cricket Club* – Brian Bearshaw
- *His own man - The life of Neville Cardus* – Christopher Brooke's
- *John Briggs (the Life of)* – Geoffrey Wolstenholme
- *Lancashire* – Rex Pogson
- *My Life -* Neville Cardus – H.G. Earnshaw
- *Old Trafford* – John Marshall
- *Play* – N.L Stevenson
- *Ranji* – Alan Ross
- *Test Cricket, volume 1. 1877 to 1939* – Roy Webber

- *Test Cricket Cavalcade (1877 to 1946)* – E.L Roberts
- *Test Cricket and Cricketers* – E.L Roberts
- *The Boundary Book (2nd innings)* – Leslie Frewin
- *The Complete History of Cricket Tours at Home and Abroad* – Peter Wynne
- *The Wars of the Roses (Cricket)* – A.A. Thomson
- *The Wisden Book of Cricket Records* – Bill Frindall

ACKNOWLEDGEMENTS

Cheadle Royal Hospital

Cheshire County Council

Don Ambrose (Cricket Historian)

Greenalls Property Management

Lancashire County Cricket Club

Leeds Central Library

Marylebone Cricket Club

Northampton Records Office

Queen Mary's Cricket Club, Walsall

Southport (Central Library)

The Book Shop - Skipton

The Cheshire Records Office

The Northern Cricket Club, Crosby, Liverpool

Widnes (Central Library)

The cartoons, originally published in the 1880s, are by RIP, who was Reginald Pretty Hill (died 1949).